'*Change Your Life, Change Your World* ... guide for personal awa[...] humanity's biggest cha[...] there for someone else [...] and it is up to each of us [...] Amoda's book shows us [...] to be an agent of change, in other words how to live a more fulfilling life while contributing to the creation of a more harmonious world.'

– Kimberly Ann Coots, Transformational Coach,
Speaker and Author

'Amoda has such magnificence to share … her light is very powerful and unique!'

– Dan Hanneman, Host of Spiritual Rock Star Radio
and Spiritual Life Coach

'For all of us who yearn for a life of freedom and a brighter future for humanity, this book shows us step by step how to be the change we seek.'

– Dr Susan Shumsky, Author, Spiritual Teacher

Amoda Maa Jeevan is a leading light and a powerful feminine voice in the new consciousness movement. She is an inspirational speaker, spiritual teacher and the author of *How to Find God in Everything*, as well as a frequent radio and TV show guest. Having been a spiritual seeker with a background in psychology for many years, in 2002 she had a mystical experience that transformed her life. Today, she offers her 'radical awakening' teaching by giving talks, workshops and retreats to a growing global audience. She currently lives in the UK with her husband, Kavi, with whom she teaches some of her retreats.

To visit Amoda's website, go to
www.AmodaMaaJeevan.com

SEP - 2012

Also by Amoda Maa Jeevan

*How to Find God in Everything: an invitation to
awaken to your true nature and transform your world*

CHANGE
YOUR
LIFE
CHANGE
YOUR
WORLD

TEN SPIRITUAL LESSONS
FOR A NEW WAY OF BEING AND LIVING

AMODA MAA JEEVAN

FOREWORD BY JOHN SELBY

WATKINS PUBLISHING
LONDON

This edition first published in the UK and USA 2012 by
Watkins Publishing, Sixth Floor, Castle House,
75–76 Wells Street, London W1T 3QH

Design and typography © Watkins Publishing 2012

Text Copyright © Amoda Maa Jeevan 2012

Amoda Maa Jeevan has asserted her right under the Copyright, Designs
and Patents Act 1988 to be identified as the author of this work.

1 3 5 7 9 10 8 6 4 2

Designed and typeset by Paul Saunders

Printed and bound in China by Imago

British Library Cataloguing-in-Publication Data Available

Library of Congress Cataloging-in-Publication Data Available

ISBN: 978-1-78028-124-7

www.watkinspublishing.co.uk

Distributed in the USA and Canada by Sterling Publishing Co., Inc.
387 Park Avenue South, New York, NY 10016-8810

For information about custom editions, special sales, premium and
corporate purchases, please contact Sterling Special Sales
Department at 800-805-5489 or specialsales@sterlingpub.com

CONTENTS

ACKNOWLEDGMENTS

Writing this book was effortless. For this I thank Divine Spirit for setting me alight with a ferocious intensity in order to give birth to a new creation in record time. I also thank my husband and beloved, Kavi Jezzie Hockaday, for his spaciousness, his vision, his enthusiasm and his unending love.

Additionally, my gratitude goes to Ed Evans whose unwavering support of my work, in so many ways, continues to be a comfort to me. To Michael Mann, my publisher, I am grateful for his capacity to believe in me. To John Selby and James Twyman – both spiritual teachers and best-selling authors I deeply respect – I am honoured and delighted by their generosity of spirit and endorsement of my work. And to the team at Watkins/Duncan Baird Publishers, I am grateful for their work behind the scenes to bring this book into your hands.

Last but certainly not least, I am immensely grateful to everyone who has hosted my talks, attended my workshops and retreats, and joined me in a growing global community dedicated to creating a more loving world … all this would be meaningless without you.

If there is anyone I have failed to mention, it is not by design but simply because the angels that surround me are too numerous to mention. My deepest gratitude goes to each and every one of you.

FOREWORD

We have reached a crisis point in our world society where we either grow up and assume full responsibility for our own thoughts and actions, or continue to plunge our world into further chaos, violence, and all the other negatives. There have been hundreds of thousands of books written about spiritual growth, mystic transformation, and social responsibility. Intellectually we now know our challenge – it's time for action, and action is what Amoda delivers in this book.

The great spiritual teacher Krishnamurti stated over and over that the world requires a major revolution; not an economic or political or religious revolution, but a psychological revolution. Even 2,500 years ago, Buddha was saying basically the same thing, and shortly thereafter Jesus was calling for a revolution not of our social or business fabric, but of our own interior beliefs and intent. What is the nature of this inner revolution, and how can we best participate?

A lasting revolution is one in which significant positive change is brought into being inside our own minds and hearts. As you'll discover in this impactful book you hold in your hands, right now you do possess the capacity for transformation; the challenge is in learning how to focus your attention in exactly the right directions to stimulate that transformation.

In order to bring about a genuine transformation of consciousness there must arise within you a commitment to regularly refocus your attention in key directions that will, step by step, wake up your inner guide and nurture genuine psychological growth. Amoda has been guided to create an excellent intergrowth program based on ten powerful refocusing themes – and the beginning point is assuming responsibility for aiming your attention with more clarity, insight, and purpose.

When beginning a serious spiritual journey such as this book offers, many people assume that there will ensue a battle between their ego and their higher spiritual self. Studying the phenomenon of meditation as a psychologist, I found this negative attitude toward one's ego entirely self-defeating. The truth is that every time you say 'I choose', it is your ego function that is stating your intent to focus in a particular direction. So it's important for your ego to mature spiritually, so that it recognizes what is most important to focus your attention upon regularly.

Spiritual awakening is all about accepting and even embracing reality. From my perspective we have had far too much mystic fantasy and ungrounded day-dreaming in the name of spiritual growth. It's time to learn how to put aside all of our imaginations, even the most beautifully mystic, and practice the essential art of seeing clearly what is real. This is the core process of Zen and all other meditation traditions worth their salt. As Lao Tzu, Buddha, Jesus, and all the rest quietly urged us over and over, we must learn how to put aside the judgmental function of the brain, so that we can actually engage with what's real.

Even though 2,000 years ago Jesus gave us the distinct order to 'Fear not', most of us are seriously uptight and worried – and this is exactly where the revolution needs to happen. We must learn how to consciously and regularly let go of all of our future worries, and regain peace in the present moment. We must take charge of our own minds – and do this not sometime in the future, but right now in this moment.

The word 'presence' has become the new buzzword in spiritual circles, and rightly so. Presence is all about being more conscious at the experiential sensory level of being. We need to practice this present-moment focusing throughout each day, if we are to act with greater clarity and inner power. Nurturing presence requires a bit of discipline in order to quiet all the inner chatter and look deeply within, listen to your inner voice of wisdom, and discover more deeply who you really are.

There is a clear process through which consciousness, step by step, expands. We tune into our core breath experience, master chronic fearful and judgmental reactions, and enter more and more often into the Silence. We can then tap into the spontaneous inflow of higher insight and unconditional compassion from our spiritual source. If we don't learn how to receive spiritual inflow, we will in fact have nothing of true value to offer the world. That's just the reality of life.

Likewise with our need to heal – physically, mentally, emotionally. We've all been damaged early in childhood. And as adults we must learn how to allow true healing to happen deep within us, so that we can act in the world with more creativity and understanding. And love is the healer – we heal when we focus our inner spiritual love over and over again exactly where we hurt inside.

There's no question about the direction of spiritual evolution related to the human brain: we have the power to choose to fixate upon fear and judgment, or upon courage and acceptance. This bears constant repeating: 'God is love'. And since love and fear are opposites, surely it is time for all of us to learn how to quiet all the anxious thoughts that continually pollute human consciousness. Only when we move progressively out of fear can we truly make a joyful noise unto the lord, and become beacons of light in the world. That's what the revolution is truly about.

Throughout Amoda's book and the entire meditative tradition is the underlying requirement of focusing upon our breath experience as often and fully as possible. We need to gently discipline ourselves to feel the air flowing in and out of the nose – right now! That simple cognitive shift is the eternal revolutionary act: become and remain fully aware of your own present-moment experience, so you remain grounded in your deeper spiritual presence no matter what you're doing.

Each new generation needs to rediscover the deeper truths of what it means to become fully human. Amoda has created an excellent new variation on the eternal human theme. I wholeheartedly welcome you to her fully enjoyable process!

JOHN SELBY
Santa Cruz, June 2011

INTRODUCTION
The Invitation
to a New Way of Being

So many of us these days are feeling the strong desire to make changes in our lives that will shift us to a new level of happiness. And so many of us are feeling the urgent call to make changes in the world that will create a brighter future for us all. This book presents the steps for creating everlasting change in your world in the only way that counts … from the inside out. I have called these steps to change 'lessons' because this is a spiritual workbook. It contains insights for contemplation and actions to take on a daily basis. Your commitment to the process will lead to a transformation of consciousness that can radically change how you see things and how you experience things. And this will have a direct impact on how you do things.

Inner transformation is the key to outer change. However much we may want to save the world or fix what's wrong, the truth remains that we change the world by changing ourselves. This book is for those of us who are tired of complaining and blaming, and instead are ready to re-create ourselves by becoming the change we want to see. It is for those of us who are ready to do what it takes to shift from smallness to greatness. Because that's what it will take to re-create our world as we wish it to be.

If you're reading this book, then you are one of those courageous souls prepared to take the leap.

THE TRANSFORMATION OF DARKNESS

The Ten Lessons outlined in this book arose out of a vision. Although this vision was transmitted to me personally several years ago, I believe it does not belong solely to me, but to each and every one of us. It is a collective vision for our times and it speaks to the inherent knowing in our hearts.

In this vision, I am walking through the Valley of Death, a place of darkness and incredible pain. With each step I feel the burden of my personal history: the emotional wounds that prevent me from opening to love, the missed opportunities in life, and the broken promises. And with each step I feel the unbearable weight of humanity's suffering: the tragedies and sicknesses that have plagued so many, and the terror of thousands of years of violence and war. I am overcome with despair and fall to the ground with a creeping coldness in my veins. Much as I struggle, I sink deeper into inertia and I know that death is close by.

As the final breath leaves my mouth, with all the strength I can muster, I find it in my heart to be grateful for the life I have been given so far. In this moment of gratitude there is a flicker of light in the distance and I am drawn towards it like a moth to a flame. I do not die but rise up to continue walking towards a golden staircase that has appeared before me. With each step I take, there is an incredible force that pulls me back towards the darkness of despair, and at the same time pulls me forward towards the hope of salvation. But neither of these options is a remedy for the pain I feel. So I choose instead to take one resolute step at a time, with absolute presence and complete surrender.

As I climb the staircase, I find that I become as naked and as innocent as a small child. And with nothing to hide, I arrive at the top and am surrounded by such a glorious light that I am convinced I have arrived at Heaven's door ... and I am ready for sweet oblivion in the arms of The Holy Father. But no sooner do I climb into His lap, than I merge with Him and I become Him. And from this place I experience the power of my Being. By my side appears The Holy Mother and I merge with Her and I become Her. And from this place I experience the compassion of my Unbounded Heart. From my womb springs a Golden Child and I experience my Divine Creative Potential. And from my breasts flows the Milk of Human Kindness that becomes the River of Life and repopulates the Valley of Death to become a Living Paradise on Earth.

What on earth could this vision mean? It took me several months to contemplate this experience. Then I understood that not only had I received an age-old wisdom that runs through all spiritual traditions, but that I had also tapped into a new evolutionary impulse that is unique to humanity's current crisis. This new evolutionary impulse is the need to grow beyond our fear so that we can bring our love into a world that is crying out for a new way of living and being.

The Valley of Death represents the 'dark night of the soul'. On a personal level, this may be a time in our lives when everything seems to be falling apart and we experience our own limitation and helplessness. Each of us may go through one or several 'dark nights' in order to shed an old skin and grow towards wholeness. Most often this is triggered by a specific, unexpected event that happens to us. But sometimes this darkness is a constant feature of our lives, especially if we have given in to the voice of doubt or despair. On a collective level, the Valley of Death refers to both the increased chaos and confusion of today's world, and the rising threat of global destruction.

The journey that ensues, from the moment the light appears in the distance, is one that describes the transformation from the samsara of small-mind thinking to the liberation of unlimited being. It is the journey that each of us is called to take in times of personal upheaval, and the one we are called to make in each moment when we step onto the path of awakening. It also describes the transformation from a world of horror to a world of glory when we make the shift from a separation-based perspective to a unity-based perspective.

So many of us are faced with increasing challenges amidst intensely turbulent times. And so many of us are seeking a way through this pain. Some of us get the sense that something new is just around the corner ... but we're not sure whether we should be excited or afraid. Change is in the air ... but we don't know whether this is for the better or for the worse. The collective vision offers us a road map through tough times. It shows us how to walk through the darkness of fear, doubt, uncertainty, and pain towards the light of our true inner radiance. It shows us that this light has the power to transform our lives from suffering to joy, and the power to transform our world from terror to peace.

And it gives us step-by-step instructions on becoming an Agent of Change.

BECOMING AN AGENT OF CHANGE

What do I mean by Agent of Change? I'm talking about someone who has the courage to take the steps to inner transformation. Someone who takes full responsibility for the experience of their life because they recognize that their outer world is always a reflection of their inner world. Someone who does what it takes to overcome self-limiting beliefs and to replace them with life-affirming choices, because they recognize that living from their highest potential is a gift to themselves and to others. And someone who dives deep inside to discover the truth of who they really are, because they recognize that only an awakened being can bring light to the world.

Very often we think that being an Agent of Change means that we need to do something to make things better, that we need to campaign to save the world, fight the good cause, fix what is wrong, or banish the enemy. But all the fighting in the world will not bring us the change we desire. It only serves to perpetuate the same fear-based paradigm that got us into the mess in the first place. To be truly effective as an Agent of Change, we need to change our internal paradigm first – our thoughts, our feelings and our beliefs. In other words, we need to change how we respond to life. Our habitual self-protective and self-serving reactions aren't working any more. We need a whole new approach.

An Agent of Change has the courage to choose a new way of being. It's a radical shift in consciousness that comes from having the tenacity to walk through the internal landscape of darkness with an open heart. The new evolutionary impulse requires our participation. We cannot sit back and wait for salvation from Heaven. We are required to consciously collaborate in our own awakening by choosing to take the inner steps to transformation. And we are required to consciously collaborate in the planetary awakening of our times through getting excited by the potential of radical change for humanity.

One person at a time is how we change the world. When each of us awakens to the miracle of our own power, we shift from being victims of our lives to being conscious co-creators. When we awaken to the power within us, we come into alignment with the power of Creation and miracles happen. But in order to awaken this power, we need to activate an inner muscle that, when used over and over again, creates ripples of remembrance in our body-mind-soul, and plugs us into the field of infinite possibilities. It is here, in the invisible realm of miraculous power, that we can choose how we want to experience our life and our world.

THE MIRACLE OF YOUR TRUE POWER

There is a miraculous force that can transform your life from the inside out. This force is the power of I AM.

Beyond all definitions of who you think you are, is a luminous presence that is rooted in the eternity of Now. It is that part of you that is forever-lasting, un-changing, and as vast as the open sky. This presence is always at one with the power of Creation; it's just that we often look for power outside of ourselves by chas-ing love, happiness, wealth and recognition from other people, things and situations. But the love, happiness, wealth and recognition we receive from outside is sub-ject to the shifting sands of time … and so it comes and goes. In other words, what we gain we are also most likely to lose. All the treasures we seek are actu-ally inside us, as part of our true divine nature. What we seek is what we are. And what we are is found by looking within.

The unchanging nature of our essential self – our I AM-ness – is available to us at all times. It is that part of us that is always at one with life as it unfolds within our own experience. It is that part of us that simply *is*. It is our Being-nature. Whatever happens in life, whatever the circumstances, we always have access to our Being-nature when we are anchored in the unfoldment of this moment *as it is*, rather than being lost in the turbulence of the thoughts in our heads.

The greatest power we have is this ability to shift from our heads to our Being-ness. It is a conscious choice that opens the door to everlasting happiness and freedom. When we make this choice, there is an alignment of our inner power with the power of the universe, and we come to know ourselves as co-creators of our reality. It is from this place that we can fulfil our divine destiny. It is from this place within ourselves that we can make all our dreams come true. True happiness and true freedom flow freely from our Being when we get ourselves out of the way.

When we are anchored in the truth of who we *really* are and not who we *think* we are, then all our actions will lead to peace, harmony, abundance and fulfilment. When we see through the unbounded clarity of our hearts instead of through the myopic perspective of the ego, then we act from our greatness instead of our smallness. Right Doing arises out of Right Being. The way through the darkness of our own fear, confusion and suffering is by shining the light of our presence on all that we think, feel, say and do. The way through the darkness of a world lost in greed, war and terror is to shine the light of our love on all that we see and hear.

The Ten Lessons outlined in the collective vision and presented in this book are a way of re-activating our true power by awakening us to our I AM-ness. Each lesson is based on a facet of our true radiant nature and activates a specific quality, or power, that creates inner and outer change. Put together, these ten qualities become like a jewel that expresses the magnificence of who we really are.

The transformation starts now ... there is no time to waste! Your life is waiting for you to awaken and re-create yourself anew. The world is waiting for each of us to awaken and become Agents of Change in the shift to a new paradigm. We stand at a crossroads and it is up to each one of us to make a choice.

We either wake up and create a new world of harmony ... or we continue to bury our heads in the sand and we fall into a world of unthinkable suffering. The future is in our hands.

THE TEN LESSONS

The Ten Lessons outlined in the following chapters are inner actions that require intention and discipline. They are based directly on the details given to me in the collective vision. After I received this transmission, I resolutely practised these lessons as I went about my daily life. Since then there has been a fundamental shift in my relationship to myself, to others, to the world, to life and to God. It has been a radical transformation that has changed everything.

The important point is that I applied these inner actions not just when I felt like it, but especially during challenging times, in moments of quiet despair, loneliness, anxiety and when things didn't go the way I wanted them to. I applied them not just as a half-hour exercise to do every day, but to every aspect of my life, from the way I was eating to the way I was feeling, and from my interactions with friends to my interactions with my bank account. The depth of my transformation was in direct proportion to the consistency of my application of these lessons.

Today, nearly ten years on, the qualities, or powers, activated by The Ten Lessons have become a natural part of who I am and how I interact with life. And yet there are times of unexpected challenge that ask me to dig deeper and exercise the inner muscle of my consciousness in ways that I had not previously imagined possible. There is no end to how much we can grow spiritually, and it is always humbling to be taken to new edges. With each new level of growth comes a renewed strength that serves to enrich not only my own life but also the lives of those around me.

By applying these Ten Lessons to your life consistently, you too will see changes take place in both your inner and outer reality. You will take your life in your hands and be empowered to be all that you dream of. But only *you* can decide if this is what you want. If it *is* what you want, then make a commitment with your whole body, mind and soul to complete the journey from Lesson One to Lesson Ten. And know that you have been called to be a part of the revolution in consciousness that has the power to change your world.

Whilst each lesson focuses on a specific power, there are certain themes that run through all of the lessons, so there will be some repetition. And whilst each lesson is complete in itself, the lessons are also cumulative, so each one builds on the previous one and gathers momentum. This is because the facets of your inner radiance cannot exist in isolation from each other. They are like the faces of a diamond; each face, or facet, is another angle from which to look at the whole. The differences in the angles create subtle variations in the view. But the light that illuminates each viewpoint emanates from one source and the full glory of what we're seeing can only reveal itself when we behold the diamond in its entirety.

I suggest immersing yourself in one lesson per week for the next ten weeks. Once you have completed all the lessons, you can always come back and repeat them to deepen your understanding. Or you can just return to whichever lesson your circumstances direct you. Each lesson includes a Daily Declaration, a Call to Action and a Self-Reflection Exercise. You will be asked to carry out all three of these exercises on a daily basis. You may wonder why you need to repeat the same exercises for seven days in a row and you may be tempted to skip some of these days. I suggest you do not. Each time you fulfil the tasks required of you, there is a deepening in both their capacity to cleanse you of toxic beliefs and to call in the light of inspiration.

You may even be tempted to just read through all the chapters and skip these exercises. But remember, this is a spiritual workbook, and without the practical application of the teachings in each chapter, there will be no embodiment of the insights offered. And so there will be no real change. You can, however, read through the whole book from cover to cover first and then come back to methodically go through the exercises for each lesson.

How to work with the Daily Declarations

The Daily Declarations are spoken statements that affirm what you desire to experience. I'm not talking about how much money you want to earn, or what kind of house you want to live in or the perfect partner you want to attract. I'm talking about what you *really* want, deep down in your soul. And what every soul really wants is to awaken to its true nature.

Words are thoughts made manifest, and carry the power of intention. By repeating affirmations within a space of relaxation and receptivity, they have the ability to penetrate the superficial layers of small mind to a deeper place in your being. At this deeper place, you are one with the power of Creation and words that resonate with this oneness will magnify this power within your life. The Daily Declarations offered in this book are affirmations of the truth of your infinite magnificence, the glory of your divinity, and the oneness of your essential nature. Each one of these affirmations includes the statement 'I AM' in order to bring you directly into the experience of your I AM-ness. They refer to the light of presence that comes when you fully step into the present moment. That's why they're written in the present tense.

Having said all this, it's important to know that affirmations are not a panacea. When I first discovered affirmations over 20 years ago, I used them obsessively, repeating positive statements all day long in the hope that they would magically make me a happier person. But without getting your hands dirty in the underworld of your subconscious, there is no authentic transformation. Without doing the inner work, affirmations become at best a spiritual band-aid. There is no replacement for honest self-inquiry. The willingness to meet your pain in the light of awareness, and to stay softly open to what is revealed, is the only effective spiritual detox programme. The Daily Declarations in this book serve not as a spiritual practice in themselves, but as a statement of your intent and a reminder of who you really are.

The potential for these affirmations to take you into the experience of your true essence comes not only when you bring your full attention to the words, but rather to the space between words. Words can only point the way, but it is in the pause between words – just as in the pause between inhale and exhale – that you discover the silence of Being. The invitation with each Daily Declaration is to take a deep breath, to relax and to allow yourself to let go into the spaciousness of silent awareness. Breathing in and breathing out, simply *be* here now. And then repeat the affirmation slowly and out aloud three times. And do this three times a day. Early morning, on rising, and just before you go to bed at night are best, along with one other time that is convenient for you. If you already have a meditation practice, you can carry out the Daily Declaration straight after this. If not, I suggest you spend at least five minutes in silence before declaring the affirmation.

How to work with the Call to Action

The core of your practice whilst working with this book is the Call to Action. Here you are asked to apply the lesson to your everyday life. Sometimes you are asked to do something tangible. At other times, you are merely asked to observe yourself as you go about your day. This part of the workbook constitutes the exercising of the inner muscle of consciousness. It's where the real transformation happens. The important thing is to be consistent throughout the day and to stay with the process in gentle resoluteness. Drop your expectations of how you should or shouldn't feel. Drop your demands of what should and shouldn't happen. A far more valuable approach is to simply and honestly be willing to meet whatever is here for you. This is the spirit of self-inquiry.

How to work with the Self-Reflection Exercise

The Self-Reflection Exercise is the opportunity to review your process throughout the day. Your review could be about what emotions arose for you, or what thoughts were prominent. It could also include any insights on the spiritual level. And even anything you experience on a bodily level.

This is the section in which you're asked to write in your journal using the blank pages at the end of each chapter. If you prefer, you can use your own special book. Allow yourself to write freely without censoring. Write as much or as little as you like. But give yourself time to be thorough. Putting words onto paper is a great way to assimilate your journey.

And finally …

It's best to have an attitude of non-attachment to the results. The important thing is to commit to the process and to take action every day. Immerse yourself in one lesson per week … repetition and persistence will sow the seeds of change. And remember that there is no failure. This is a journey of self-inquiry, and the light of awareness always sends torchlight into the deeper recesses of our psyches where unconscious patterns lay buried. There may be times when the journey seems uphill and you doubt whether any real change for the better is happening. The process of transformation is like lighting a fire – you need to be gentle but consistent. Trust that the spark you ignite now, through your efforts, will burst into the flame of awakening.

Let us begin the journey …

TEN SPIRITUAL
LESSONS

RESPONSIBILITY
The Power to Make a Choice

You cannot control what happens in your life, but you can be in charge of how you perceive and respond to what happens. As soon as you accept 100 per cent responsibility for your thoughts, feelings and actions, you are no longer a victim of circumstance; instead you are empowered to be a co-creator of your reality.

There is a famous Zen story about a farmer and his son that encapsulates with elegant simplicity the wisdom of this first lesson.

The farmer lived in the days when there was frequent fighting between small kingdoms in China. The farmer had a son who was tilling a small field with the help of his horse. One day the horse ran away. The neighbours heard about this and came to the farmer's house to commiserate. 'We are so very sorry,' they cried, 'this is a very bad situation. You have such bad luck.' The farmer simply said, 'Maybe.' The next day the horse came back and brought with it half a dozen other wild horses. The neighbours came round again, this time to rejoice. 'This is such good news,' they said, 'what tremendous luck.' The farmer said, 'Maybe.' On the third day the son fell and broke his leg while trying to ride one of the wild horses. The neighbours came round yet again, crying and wailing about what bad luck it was. The farmer said, 'Maybe.' The next day the king's people came to recruit strong healthy farmers into the army. When they found the farmer's son with a broken leg they left him alone. The neighbours came again and gave a huge sigh of relief. They said it wasn't such bad luck after all and that everything had turned out well. The farmer said, again, 'Maybe.'

You see, we really can't control what happens. The nature of life itself is change. The old farmer in the story clearly has the wisdom to know that events are unpredictable and impermanent. He also has the wisdom to know that whatever the circumstances of our lives, we have a choice in how we respond to what happens. We are each 100 per cent responsible for our thoughts, feelings and actions.

As long as you believe that someone or something outside of you is responsible for how you feel, you remain disempowered. As long as you blame other people, events, the world, life, God – or yourself – when things don't turn out the way you want them to, you remain a victim of circumstance. And as long as your happiness – and your unhappiness – is dependent on external circumstances, you remain a victim of life.

The first step in becoming an Agent of Change is recognizing that you *do* have a choice in how you respond to what happens; what you choose to think, choose to feel and choose to do creates your reality ... for better or for worse. You're either living a radiant life in which the magnificence of your essential being remains untarnished by the changing nature of things ... or you're playing it small by giving your power away to external circumstances. The former means that nothing has the power to take away your inner peace. The latter means you are run ragged by the vicissitudes of life.

Empowering yourself to choose how you respond to what's happening liberates you from being a victim of circumstance. I know this is often very difficult to believe, and all the more difficult to put into action, in the midst of intense emotion or extreme suffering. But just being willing to even consider that you have the choice to respond differently opens the door to a new possibility. I invite you to consider right here and *now* – if you haven't done so already – that it is not the circumstances of your life that make you sad or angry or frustrated, but that *you* are choosing to be sad or angry or frustrated. I invite you to consider that it is not your life that is making you unhappy, but that *you* are choosing to be unhappy. And I invite you to consider the possibility that you can choose differently. Right here and *now*, I invite you to consider that you can choose to respond in a way that totally changes the way you see things.

The way we *see* things is the crucial point here, because it is also the way we *experience* things. Our reality is created by our core beliefs about ourselves, about others, about the world, about life and about God. By the way, you can replace the word God here with Goddess, Spirit, or any other word that is appropriate for you; we've all got core beliefs about this even if we don't believe in God or a higher power. A core belief is the lens we look through to see the world. It's created by giving our attention to a particular thought – and to the feeling that follows this thought – over and over again. We don't actually see things as they are but as we *think* and *feel* them to be. These thoughts and feelings are so ingrained that we believe we're seeing reality. It's like being in a goldfish bowl in which you're the goldfish swimming round in circles believing this is how the world is. But what you're really seeing – and experiencing – is a tiny snapshot of the bigger picture … because you haven't yet taken the leap into freedom.

Core beliefs live below the surface of our everyday waking mind, so they are difficult to see. But there's an in-built universal mechanism that never fails to reveal the truth. Every interaction you have in your daily life reflects back to you what you believe about yourself, about others, about the world, about life and about God. The outer world, as we perceive and experience it, always mirrors our inner world because we live in a vibrational world. Every single thing that exists is made up energy. Energy is partly measured by the frequency – in other words, the speed – of the wave being created. So every single thing that exists, vibrates at a certain frequency. This includes everything that is alive and everything that is man-made. And it includes every thought and every feeling.

Each of us also has a personal vibration that is made up of the overall frequency of our habitual thoughts and feelings. It's like an invisible note that resounds from our core and sends ripples of energy throughout our lives. This personal vibration has a direct impact on both our internal and external environments. As this wave travels inwards it impacts every cell of our physical body, every neurone that fires, every thought and every emotion. As it travels outwards it impacts the people we meet, the activities we are involved in, and the world around us. The effect of our personal vibration on our internal and external environments has been scientifically tested using thousands of individuals over several decades. In his seminal book, *Power vs. Force*, Dr David Hawkins documents the results of these studies which unequivocally show that low-vibration thoughts and feelings, such as fear and hate, weaken the body and create discord in our environment, whilst high-vibration thoughts and feelings, such as love and compassion, strengthen the body and create harmony in our environment.

We also live in a magnetic world. Not only do we send a wave of energy out into our environment, but we call towards ourselves people, events and situations that match our vibrational frequency. Habitual thoughts and feelings of limitation and unworthiness attract circumstances that confirm our sense of limitation and unworthiness. Conversely, habitual thoughts and feelings of expansion and self-worth attract circumstances that confirm these senses. Although it's not quite as simple as saying that if we focus on positive thoughts and feelings we'll attract good things into our life, whilst focus on negative thoughts and feelings will attract bad things. There's a subtlety to the universal law of attraction that often gets missed. You can think all the positive thoughts you like, and you can affirm all the good things you'd like to have, but unless there's a congruency between what you *want* and how you *really* think and feel about yourself, then your unexamined core beliefs eventually sabotage your happiness.

Consider for a moment that you have the core belief '*I am not good enough*' running like a tape loop through your subconscious mind. When I worked as a breath-work therapist and emotional-release counsellor, this was the one core belief I witnessed most frequently. Honest inquiry will most likely reveal that you too have this belief – or some variation of it – embedded in your energy-system. It's so common because it has its roots in the separation from our divine wholeness. '*I am not good enough*' leads to the feeling of shame because you deem yourself to be imperfect. Shame means you draw down the shutters on the brilliance of your radiant nature. And since you are a vibrational and a magnetic being, what you give is what you get. The refusal to recognize and reveal the light of your own magnificence draws towards you situations and people that do not value you. However much you may consciously want to be successful and fulfilled, your unexamined belief of not being good enough continues to be affirmed.

You may then react by being angry at the world for not being good enough, or for being imperfect because it does not give you what you want. This reinforces your low personal vibration of unworthiness and so it goes on. You go round and round like the goldfish in the bowl, believing that this is how things are.

My personal take on this used to be '*I am unloveable*', and this meant I couldn't love myself. Since I couldn't love myself, I couldn't really love the man I was with: you can't give someone else what you can't give yourself. As in the previous example, what you give is what you get. Or in this case, what you don't give is what you don't get! The love I was unable to extend to this man was in exact proportion to the love he didn't show me … at least not in the form I thought it should come in. I spent many years blaming him for being unloving, when all along it was me who was being unloving towards myself. What I've just described here is a relationship based on need rather than real love. It's called a co-dependent relationship and it's what the majority of people think of as normal.

What all this says is that our reality is a creation of our own personal vibration; what we see and experience is a reflection of the frequency of our consciousness. As *A Course in Miracles* says: '*Projection makes perception*'. Another way of saying this is: '*We look inside first, decide what kind of world we want to see and then project that onto the world outside, believing it the truth as we see it'*. We go about our lives thinking that *we* exist inside the world. But it is more accurate to say that *the world* exists inside us. This is such a powerful statement to understand. It's a turnaround in perception that takes us to a whole new level of maturity by giving us the power of responsibility. From this new standpoint, instead of blaming our biology for an overweight body, we are now empowered to examine our beliefs about ourselves and to see how weighty thoughts and feelings have created an unwholesome condition. And instead of blaming the economy for the black hole of personal debt, we are now empowered to examine our beliefs about the world, and to see how impoverished thoughts and feelings have created a situation of lack in our lives. These are just two common examples of how taking responsibility for our own unhappiness frees us from victim-hood.

The ability to create your life as you wish it to be requires that you become a master of your inner world. It requires that you recognize that you are the author of your reality and that you examine your erroneous perceptions; and then that you take a leap into a whole new way of seeing things. It's a radically different perspective in which you stop being a victim of your own mind and become its master. It goes way beyond your judgments of right and wrong because it transcends duality and ushers you into a whole new way of experiencing things.

In the Zen story, the farmer does not label the events that happen as either good or bad. His perception is not tainted by wanting things to be this way or that way; his inner peace is not dependent on what happens. It's not the events themselves that matter but the way we see them. Many times, what appears to be a calamity turns out to be exactly what we need, whether on a material, emotional or spiritual level. Wisdom is the ability to see the bigger picture and not get lost in what we reactively label as good or bad. Freedom is the capacity to see the offering of divinity in everything that happens.

The choice to see divinity grants you the power of being a co-creator. It engages you with the co-creative power of existence and aligns your will with Divine Intention. In this alignment there's a congruency between how you choose to respond to life – your thoughts, feelings and actions – and the unfolding process of life. Therefore, you and God are working together instead of opposing each other. This beautiful paradox of taking responsibility for how you respond to life whilst giving it up to a higher power is the key to your empowerment.

This first lesson lays the foundation for everything else that follows. Without this first step, you have no ground to walk on. In the collective vision, this first step is the decision to rise up from the Valley of Death and follow the light. It's the activation of personal will that brings you into engagement with your divine destiny. Like all the other steps that you are invited to take, as you climb the golden staircase to the revelation of your true divine nature, this is an ongoing conscious choice to walk steadfastly through the darkness of fear towards the radiance of love.

The power to make a conscious choice in how you respond to life is an inner muscle that requires you to practise over and over again. There is no quick fix. But there is the promise of a whole new world of possibilities in which you can re-create your life from the inside out. Everything you desire is within you. Love, happiness, peace and abundance are the treasures of your inner nature.

Harnessing this power means you sow the seeds for real change. Real change in your life. And real change in the world. When your actions are rooted in the deeper truth of your co-creative nature, then everything that you do will have a far-reaching impact. It's in our interest to create now what future generations will need in order to survive the dramatic changes that are sweeping through our planet. If we get it right, we may even do better than mere survival. This could be the flowering of a new humanity in which we thrive in ways we cannot yet fully comprehend.

The question is, are you willing to take the leap out of the goldfish bowl and set yourself free? If the answer is *yes* … read on.

DAILY DECLARATION

Repeat 3 times daily

I AM a co-creator of my life.

I choose my thoughts, my feelings, my words and my actions.

I AM the master of my inner world.

Everything I desire – all the love, happiness, peace and abundance – is within me.

And I choose thoughts and feelings of love, happiness, peace and abundance whatever the circumstances.

I have the power to make a conscious choice in every moment.

CALL TO ACTION

Today you will make – should you choose to take up the invitation – perhaps the most important decision of your life. It is the decision to no longer be a victim of circumstances. Whether you blame events that happened in the past for your current state of unhappiness or discontent, or whether you are fearful of what may happen in the future because it may not be the way you want it, you can decide now – in *this* very moment – that you will stop giving your power away to that which you cannot control.

Decide *today* that you will empower yourself to choose how you respond to life. Know that no-one and no-thing has the power to make you think or feel anything you don't want to think and feel. Know that you can choose to be at peace with all that *has* happened, all that *will* happen and all that *is* happening. You may not like any of these events, but that is of no real consequence, because liking and disliking are reactions that have no basis in truth. Far more real and far more powerful is the peace that is your essential nature. It is that part of you that is not rocked by external events. Recognize that this peace is ever-present – it always *has* been and always *will* be – whatever is happening. And choose to be anchored here within this peace.

Your decision to take total responsibility for how you respond to life gives you the power of inner mastery. Ask yourself: '*Is this not what I truly want?*' If the answer is an honest *yes* – even though you may not yet believe in your own mastery – then you have sown the seeds of becoming a co-creator of your life. And, just like a seed, this new way of being needs tender care. It needs your attention and your patience in order to fully sprout and bear fruit.

The garden of your consciousness also requires weeding, as old patterns of thinking and feeling will try to keep a hold. Awareness – just like light and just like love – always brings up anything unlike itself in order to be seen and released. So as you bring your attention to life-affirming new choices, there will be an equal and opposite emergence of self-limiting beliefs that were previously buried in the dark. This is a good sign. It means the process of clearing out the old and calling in the new is in motion. Your task here is to simply be vigilant, to observe without self-condemnation; to gently but resolutely decide that you will no longer be a victim of what does not serve your highest potential.

It's a decision that requires constant renewal and this is the whole purpose of the Call to Action in Lesson One: to start exercising an inner muscle that activates your will. Decide *now* that you are a master of your inner world. And promise yourself that you will make this decision *every day* for the next seven days … and keep making this decision every day from here on!

SELF-REFLECTION EXERCISE

At the end of each day, take a few minutes to reflect on the day's events and to write in your journal. Reflect on the people you interacted with, the places you went, and the circumstances you were in. And reflect on your thoughts, feelings and actions in response to these situations. Did you feel like a victim or did you take 100 per cent responsibility for your response? As you go through the day in your mind, these may be particularly useful questions to ask yourself:

✦ To whom or to what did you give your power?

✦ Of whom or of what are you a victim?

✦ On whom or on what is your happiness and inner peace dependent?

Have no judgment towards yourself, simply observe and be truthful. Know that you are taking care of your garden and that, in time, it will grow into something glorious.

JOURNAL PAGES

....

....

....

....

....

....

....

....

....

....

....

....

....

....

....

....

....

....

....

....

....

....

....

....

....

....

....

....

....

....

....

....

....

....

....

....

CLARITY
The Power to See

Identify your story-lines and you will see clearly. Recognize your erroneous perception and you will have true vision and peace.

The recognition that the world you experience is a reflection of your inner world gives birth to the most precious tool for becoming an Agent of Change. This tool is awareness, which has the ability to shift you from reaction to response.

Put simply, awareness is the power to see with clarity. To see things *as they are*, not as you think and feel them to be. But before you can see things as they are, you need to become aware of what clouds your vision. I call this '*identifying your story-lines*'.

A story-line is exactly what it says it is. It is a statement you make to yourself – about yourself, about others, about the world, about life and about God – that is not the truth even though you may think it is. In other words, it's a story … it's an imagined truth. It may be true according to the way you see things, but it's not true according to the way things really are. How can you identify a story-line? By recognizing that it always involves a degree of judgment, attack, defence or self-pity; and always leads to blame, shame, pain or complaint.

Some of the most common story-lines are:

✦ '*I shouldn't have done that, I must be a bad person.*' This leads to shame.

✦ '*You shouldn't have done that, you must be a bad person.*' This leads to blame.

✦ '*Things never work out the way I want them to, poor me.*' This leads to complaint.

✦ '*God shouldn't have let this happen, it must be a bad world.*' This leads to pain.

I invite you to take a moment to reflect on each of the above statements. Do you notice how they each have something in common?

Each of these statements contains three stages of experience:

1. *A thought based on something experienced in the past.*

Taking the first story-line listed above, the thought '*I shouldn't have done that*' is based on the memory that when I did this in the past, I experienced pain of some kind.

2. *A feeling based on a projection into the future.*

Using the same story-line as our example, the feeling is likely to be one of anxiety that I will experience pain again.

And most crucially of all …

3. *Both the thought and the feeling contaminate the present.*

Based on the previous two stages, I now conclude that the pain must be a punishment and therefore I must be a bad person. This conclusion has the effect of bringing shame into present moment reality. And shame has the immediately gratifying effect of shielding me from feeling the full extent of my pain in this moment. But it is also like a heavy cloud that blocks out the sunshine of my essential nature.

This erroneous way of seeing things cannot possibly lead to peace. It can only lead to stress – the inability to be present to what is. It's a result of dwelling in the remembrance of what went wrong in the past and then running ahead to make sure it won't go wrong in the future. The fabrication of a story-line is an attempt to protect yourself from the full depth of your agony when things don't turn out the way you want them to.

This is the way we've been trained to relate to life. Our family, our schooling, our society and our culture have all conspired to create an environment in which self-protection is paramount. As children we learnt that responding to circumstances with certain thoughts and feelings prevented us from being hurt or abandoned, either emotionally or physically. It's these habitual thoughts and feelings that become the core beliefs that cloud the way we see things. It's a primitive survival mechanism with its roots in our evolutionary conditioning. We've all inherited deep in our genes a 'fight or flight' response. Once upon a time it prevented us from being eaten alive. Today it prevents us from evolving beyond fear.

We live at a time in which the impulse is to grow into our greatness. We can't do that if we're stuck in victimhood. The grandeur of our divine destiny demands that we take an honest look at our story of 'poor me' and see it for what it is – a lie based on the notion that we are separate from All That Is. It's a serious flaw of perception that serves no other purpose than to perpetuate our suffering.

If you can honestly say that you've had enough of this suffering, you can now take the next step on the journey of transforming your world. This is the application of the tool of awareness. Awareness is the doorway to truth. And truth is what sets you free.

The first thing to do is to notice how you feel. Feelings are often easier to notice than thoughts. This is because a feeling always comes after a thought therefore it's closer to the surface of your experience. You can tell when you're stuck in victim-hood because you feel anxious, tense, afraid, angry, resentful, jealous, envious, isolated or lonely. Even a whisper of these feelings means there is a story-line attached to whatever is happening.

Once you've noticed how you feel, delve a little deeper by noticing what thoughts are playing themselves out in your head. This is the part called '*identifying your story-lines*'. Notice any thoughts of justification, attack, defence or self-pity. By identifying your story-lines, you loosen the power of their grip.

Once you've identified your story-lines, simply stop. Take a breath. And ask yourself: '*What is true here?*' The effect of asking this one simple question is like piercing the veil to reveal a clearer picture of reality. You'll see that what you've been telling yourself is the truth, and what is truly happening, are at odds with each other – the story-lines in your head and the reality of how things are in the present simply don't match up.

Story-lines are essentially thoughts. Inevitably there is a feeling attached, but the bare bones of a story-line comprise a thought. And thoughts are like clouds that pass in the sky. When you look closely at clouds they start to evaporate. It's the same with thoughts; when you look through the clear lens of awareness, they lose their urgency and dissolve. That's because story-lines are based on the past and on the future. And since the past died a long time ago and the future is yet to be born, neither of these can actually exist. Time is an illusion created by ego. The only reality there is, exists in this very moment.

So the trick here is to identify the story-lines but not to identify with them. You *have* thoughts but *you* are *not* your thoughts. This is what I have already referred to as becoming a master of your inner world.

The recognition that the thoughts in your head neither represent who you really are nor the truth of how things are, clears the lens of your consciousness. This new view affords you the freedom to see the world unencumbered by self-limiting beliefs. It's an unclut-tered space in which there is not only clarity of vision but also a profound inner silence. This is not the silence borne out of the cessation of life, but an attunement to the source of life. It's a stilling of ego's chatter to allow a quiet but absolutely powerful voice to be heard.

This voice is the sound of I AM; that part of you that is connected to the infinite flow of Divine Intelligence. This voice is always loving, joyful, peaceful and abun-dant. And it always has your highest good in mind. It comes in the form of a whisper of intuition, guiding you in the right direction. It comes to you as a spark of inspiration lighting up your day. It comes to you as the invisible embrace of upliftment that writes a gentle smile on your face. And it comes to you as the inaudible applause in your heart for simply being alive.

The recognition of the voice of I AM leads you to the discovery that you are far more powerful than you had ever imagined. No longer shackled by the limitations of your story-lines, you are released to be all that you truly are. You are, in fact, the vast open spaciousness of Being. You are as unbounded as the sky and as eter-nal as existence. In this space of clear Being, you have the power to choose thoughts aligned to your highest truth. And your highest truth is always at one with the power of Divine Mind.

The power to see with clarity erases all inner and outer conflict, and bestows upon us the blessing of inner and outer peace. We are no longer at war with ourselves nor with anyone else, because now there is a congruency between our inner being and our outer doing. Resting in the truth of presence, we are at peace with the present. There is no longer the need to fight what is happening, nor the need to defend ourselves from what might hurt, nor attack that which we perceive to be wrong or bad.

All arguments, all fights and all wars arise out of ignorance. And ignorance arises from a mistaken belief in separation. It's a blind spot that has blighted humanity for millennia. A new vision will be gained when each of us recognizes that separation is an illusion created by the ego. Then we will return to our true nature as peace.

And a new world of peace will be born.

DAILY DECLARATION

Repeat 3 times daily

I choose to enter my mind with the light of awareness.

I choose to live my life in the truth of now.

I AM at peace with myself and at peace with the world.

CALL TO ACTION

Piercing the clouds of past-fear and future-hope with the light of your awareness is a choice that requires the reactivation of your commitment in every moment. There will, of course, be moments when you forget. There's a tendency we all have to beat up on ourselves when we get it wrong. But metaphorical self-flagellation serves nothing other than to make you feel more victimized. If you notice that you are lost in the past or in the future, then gently but resolutely bring your awareness right *here* into the present. The mere fact that you have noticed your forgetfulness is a sign that you are strengthening the muscle of awareness.

The Call to Action for Lesson Two is the commitment to observe what you are thinking and what you are feeling. Make a commitment – each morning and each evening this week as well as at any other time during your day, especially when stressed – to ask yourself how you are feeling. Do you feel tense, anxious, resentful, depressed, alienated? Then take a few moments to identify the thought behind this feeling. And ask yourself: '*Is this true?*' With your attention on the thought, keep asking yourself this question until you can see that this is just a story-line that is not the truth of how things are in this very moment.

Now ask yourself if you are willing to release your attachment to this thought? Can you allow yourself to simply be without a story-line? Can you just *be*? Can you feel some spaciousness, lightness, etc?

Initially, it may be quite hard to let go, but with practice you'll be able to identify and let go of your story-lines as they happen. See them as clouds passing in an open sky. Neither resist nor chase them. Simply let them float by whilst you remain anchored in the spaciousness of Being.

It's helpful to have two 5-minute sessions devoted to this practice – one at the start of your day and one at the end of your day. In these short sessions, close your eyes and scan your mind for any story-lines. Just by shining the light of your awareness on your mind, your favourite story-lines will be revealed. Throughout the day, simply stay vigilant to how you are feeling and apply this practice when you are feeling stress or discomfort in any way.

SELF-REFLECTION EXERCISE

At the end of each day, take a few minutes to reflect and write down your observations. Ask yourself these questions:

◆ What feelings were most prevalent?

◆ What story-lines were most prevalent?

◆ Were you able to let them go or was it a struggle?

◆ If you were able to let them go, how did you feel?

Remember, there is no right or wrong way to answer these questions. Your honest inquiry is all that matters. The more you shine the light of your awareness onto what is happening in your mind, the clearer the lens of your consciousness will become. The time it takes to self-reflect is worth a thousand suns!

JOURNAL PAGES

....

....

....

....

....

....

....

....

....

....

....

....

....

....

....

....

....

....

....

....

....

....

....

....

....

....

....

....

....

....

....

....

....

....

....

....

....

....

....

....

....

....

....

....

....

RELAXATION
The Power to Let Go

*When things get tough, recognize your closure
and practise softening into the edges.*

Have you ever watched a tree, swaying in a gust of wind? Or a duck, bobbing along the current of a river? If you watch long enough, you'll feel a sense of peace arise within you. And the longer you watch, the more likely you are to notice that this peacefulness is also in the tree and in the duck. This peace is a state of deep relaxation.

Relaxation is our natural state. It's also the state of all things in nature. Relaxation is the power to let go, to yield to the changing tides of life. Contrary to mainstream belief, the ability to yield is not a weakness but a great strength. A martial artist has mastered the art of yielding; he works with the forces of Nature not against them. Watch how a practitioner of chi kung, for instance, exhibits incredible physical power and yet every fibre of his being is incredibly relaxed. This concept has been taken to an extreme in movies such as *The Matrix*, in which Neo demonstrates supernatural abilities by practising the skill of meeting attack with the power of yielding.

The opposite of relaxation is resistance. Imagine a tree resisting the wind – it would snap in two. Imagine a duck fighting against the river – it would paddle furiously and get nowhere. But this is what most of us do in the face of adversity. We resist what feels difficult, challenging or painful. Our most common reaction to what we don't like is to harden, to tighten, to contract. Or else we shut down, we become numb, we space out. But this closure doesn't make the pain go away. It doesn't make things better. It simply prolongs the agony. It really *is* a case of 'what you resist persists'.

Resistance means you fight the flow of life. You reject reality. You argue with what is. In resistance, you move away from the full depth of this moment as it unfolds within your own experience. And in moving away from this moment, you contract to fit the shell of your ego. The ego has a horror of change. It neither likes nor wants it, and will do whatever it can to prevent it. Change spells the unknown, and the unknown sets off alarm bells to the ego. Millennia ago, this was a valid response. When the pace of life was slow and everyday routine revolved around basic physical needs, the ego performed a vital function in protecting us from immediate danger. But today things are dramatically different. Life is furiously fast and our needs have, for the most part, transcended rudimentary survival. Today, we are collectively at the leading edge of an evolutionary transition that requires us to grow emotionally, mentally and spiritually. And growth demands the capacity and the desire to embrace change.

Ego's refusal to embrace change limits us from taking the next evolutionary step into daring to be all that we truly are. What we truly are is magnificent, radiant, limitless and free. But these facets of our inner jewel cannot shine through our thoughts, feelings, words and actions if they are covered up by defensive structures. The ego sees its job as the engineer of these structures. Every time it sees a threat, it designs and erects a wall between what is on the outside and what is on the inside. This happens whether the threat is real, as in the case of a large truck coming towards you as you cross the road ... or whether it is imaginary, as in the case of that long-awaited invitation to speak in front of a large audience. The wall is the story you create about it. It's the resistance – the doubt, the procrastination, the complaint; it's the ifs, buts and maybes.

Every story of '*I can't*', '*I won't*' and '*I'm not ready*' moves you several more degrees away from the openness of your essential nature. You move away from the natural peace of your Being-ness and get caught up in the noise in your head. Until eventually you can't remember who you truly are. This is the state most people find themselves in. No wonder anxiety, depression and a sense of alienation are a symptom of the modern age.

The mental and emotional suffering so many people experience is a direct result of ego's strategy of putting up a barrage of defensive walls in order to keep you in here, and everything else out there. The greater the distance between *you* and *me*, between *you* and *the world*, between *you* and *life*, and between *you* and *God*, the greater your suffering. Separation – not pain – is the root cause of all suffering.

The way through this suffering is to recognize your closure and to practise softening into the edges. The recognition of your closure brings awareness into the present, and the ego cannot continue its fight in the presence of awareness. When you're faced with a challenging situation, instead of protecting yourself from the fullness of whatever you are experiencing, soften into it and feel it even more fully. Instead of pushing life away because you don't like what it's offering you, practise letting go of resistance and allowing life to wash through you and over you. Instead of grasping tightly onto life because you're frightened of what comes next and you don't want things to change, practise softening your stranglehold. The invitation is to allow life to follow its own rhythm. The invitation is to allow life to flow like a river.

My invitation to you – right here and *now* – is to imagine a situation that challenges you or feels painful. Become aware of how you, perhaps, want to shut down or turn away. Become aware of how, perhaps, your body and your mind tighten against the experience. Now rein in the desire to move away from the imaginary pain. Make a decision to be present to what is. Simply take in a soft inhalation and release a soft exhalation. Simply relax and be OK with how it is.

The more deeply you relax and allow life to unfold in its depth and breadth, the more your body, mind and soul will be nourished. Relaxation allows every cell of your being to receive the goodness that is available from Divine Source. There is an invisible energy that permeates everything – even what we call 'empty space' – and it is this energy that ultimately sustains us. This invisible blueprint of Creation is always perfect.

When we relax enough to allow its flow into our lives, we experience an unlimited sense of well-being.

Another way of saying this is that letting go of resistance has the power to transform the misery of being closed to the miracle of openness. The misery of feeling disconnected, purposeless, or struggling to get what you want from life, is a reflection of your closure. As Lesson One shows us, our outer world always mirrors our inner world. The more you shut down, the less life has to offer you. The less you allow yourself to be touched by life's full array of experiences, the less life reaches out to touch you with the depth of its meaning.

It is not the depth of your feeling that hurts, but the strength of your resistance. Feeling something fully will not kill you. But tightening so hard that you don't feel it at all most likely will. Tightening creates stress and stress creates dis-ease. Tension in the body affects every single organ. It especially affects the heart and can lead to cardiovascular health problems. Tension in the mind creates unhappiness. And the suppression of feelings in order to avoid discomfort creates a suppression of the immune system in the body that weakens your physical, mental and emotional response to stressful situations. The more you push down what you don't want to feel, the more the build-up of toxic emotions. It then takes only a minor trigger to send you reeling back into hell.

Relaxing and flowing with the contours of what hurts, opens a doorway to a whole new level of experience. It hurts much less when you take a deep breath and soften around your pain instead of tightening against it. The softening is what allows the ego's defensive wall to dissolve. In the collective vision, it's only when I stopped fighting against the possibility of death that a glimmer of light appeared and a transformational journey began. In letting myself go into the deepest fear any human being can have – the fear of total annihilation – I was reborn into my greatness.

It's such an important point that I have to say it again: the ego cannot exist in the present. Relaxation brings you into the present so that what lies beneath and beyond your ego can be revealed. What is revealed is the majesty of your true nature.

Your true nature is unlimited and unafraid. Your true nature is like a flower whose petals open to receive both the sunshine and the rain. A flower does not divide its experience into good or bad. A flower does not resist life – it is at one with what is. In true acceptance of this moment as it unfolds, your pain becomes a doorway to a deeper relationship with life. In bringing the depth of your presence to the agony of what is presenting itself to you, your suffering turns into the blessing of intimacy with what is. Gone will be the feeling of alienation. Gone will be the sense of meaninglessness. Gone will be the anxiety and depression. Life will no longer be something that happens *to* you, but something that happens *through* you. You and life will be one. And so whatever happens is OK. How can it be otherwise, if life simply *is* what is?

The more you let go and relax, the closer you get to the joy of at-onement. The power to let go gives you the freedom to be who you really are. The natural by-product of this freedom is the release of the sweet fragrance of your essence. Just like a flower, there is no discrimination; this fragrance is available to all who come into your vicinity. And it's available to everyone and to everything that exists. There is no concern for who or what might be the most deserving of the purity of your emanation. There is no striving to reach someone or something. There is no inner conflict. There is simply the joy of Being. Joy is your essential nature. It connects you to such a sense of aliveness that you simply enjoy being alive. And others enjoy being around you. It does not matter what you do or what you don't do. What matters is the space from which doing or not-doing arises.

Taking action in a state of inner resistance creates a reluctance or lacklustre to what we do. We'd rather not be doing it. Worse still, we may hate doing it. This level of negativity sets up disharmony in the very fabric of creation and has direct repercussions on our personal life. Resistance on the inside is always met with resistance on the outside. Frustration, setbacks and mistakes are a sign that we are out of sync with the natural order of things. And the natural order of things is a state of deep relaxation.

Taking action from a place of inner relaxation joins the forces of our spirit with the creative energies of existence. In this holy communion, we enter a world of miracles in which synchronicities, opportunities and a sense of divine flow become the bedrock of our everyday experience.

This is the power of co-operation – the strength that comes from joining forces. It is a unification of inner and outer energies that leads to unity in the heart as well as unity in the world.

Imagine a world populated by six billion relaxed people. Imagine each of these six billion people is at one with themselves and at one with life. Imagine each one of them radiating with joy. Perhaps that's too much of a stretch for the imagination right now. Imagine 1,000 instead … or even just 100. What a sense of unity would arise! What a sense of upliftment!

The dream of a united humanity can become a reality if we each, as individuals, choose to take the leap from the prison of ego into the spaciousness of Being.

DAILY DECLARATION

Repeat 3 times daily

I choose to soften the contours of my consciousness and simply be here now.

I relax my breath, I relax my body, I relax my mind.

I allow life to flow through me like a river.

I choose to let go and let God.

In this perfect moment, I AM at one with myself and at one with what is.

CALL TO ACTION

This week you will practise letting go. Take a piece of paper and a brightly coloured pen and make a sign to remind yourself. Write: '*I Breathe and I Let Go*'. Place this sign on your desk, on your fridge, on your bathroom mirror … wherever you will see it. Even better, make several signs and place them everywhere.

As you go about your day, notice your closure when things don't go quite the way you want them to, or expect them to. Notice how your body tenses up, how your mind tightens into '*I can't*' or '*I won't*'. And every time you notice this – and here is the important part – take a pause in whatever you're doing. Simply *stop* – and it only takes a moment to inhabit this space of stopping – and choose to meet whatever resistance you're feeling with a gentle openness.

Now breathe in deeply and softly, allowing yourself to get closer to the knot of resistance. And breathe out deeply and softly, allowing the edges of this knot to simply melt away. Do you notice how you can't be caught up in stressful thoughts when you are breathing consciously? Breath has the power to bring us right here into the present moment. It's a moment in which all resistance dissolves into nothingness.

As in the previous lesson, I suggest you commit to two 5-minute practice sessions, morning and evening, in which you focus specifically on breathing away any stress or tension. This is in addition to the vigilance required throughout the day.

SELF-REFLECTION EXERCISE

At the end of each day, reflect and write in your journal. Describe how you practised letting go of resistance. Describe where you met with resistance and how it felt … was it in your body, in your mind or in your emotions? Was it easy or difficult to let go? And how did you feel when you did let go?

Allow your writing to flow freely without censorship. Breathe and let go as you write, allowing deeper insights to emerge into the light of your awareness.

JOURNAL PAGES

....

....

....

....

....

....

....

....

....

....

....

....

....

....

....

....

....

....

....

....

....

....

....

....

....

....

....

....

....

....

PRESENCE
The Power to Know Who You Are

Penetrate this moment, exactly as it is, with the depth of your presence and you will experience the radiance of your true power.

There's such a tendency to avoid the full depth of our experience by looking elsewhere for something to make us feel better about ourselves. We can spend a lifetime searching for relationships, recognition, security or things to fill up the hole inside. And all the time we forget that we are already whole.

The thing is, everything that we seek to gain from external sources is subject to the law of rise and fall. In other words, what we gain we also inevitably lose. Romantic love, money, status, possessions … all these things come and go. Even a millionaire eventually dies with nothing. And even a mountain eventually erodes to dust. Everything we experience through our five senses – everything we see, hear, touch, taste and smell – is transient. And that which is transient cannot possibly be truly powerful.

Your greatness is found not by chasing your dreams of a perfect life nor by running away from what scares you, but by anchoring yourself deeply in *this* moment and *each* moment as it unfolds. By penetrating this moment exactly *as it is* with the depth of your presence, you experience your true power.

Your true power is that which is not subject to the vicissitudes of small-mind thinking nor to the shifting sands of time. It is that which is not rocked by the changing nature of external events. It is that which is not tarnished by fleeting moods nor tainted by turbulent thoughts. It is that part of you which remains when everything falls apart. It is that part which remains when everything you have is taken away from you. And it is that part which remains when you're stripped bare of who you think you are.

Your true power is your eternal unchanging consciousness. It is that within which everything else comes and goes.

What I'm referring to here is the wide-open space of awareness. You can also call it the forever-present witness. It is your Being-ness. Your I AM-ness. Let's get clear here … this I AM-ness is neither 'I am *this*' nor is it 'I am *that*'. It's neither '*I am rich*' nor '*I am poor*'. Neither is it '*I am a success*' nor '*I am a failure*'. And it certainly isn't '*I am happy*' or '*I am unhappy*'. It's not even '*I am a woman*' or '*I am a man*'. We could go on here, but I think you get the point. It is simply I AM. And it is right *here* that your power lies.

Your true power lies not in what you *do* or what you *have*, but in the ability to shift from seeing through the eyes of ego to seeing through the eyes of Being. It is the ability to root yourself in the unbounded clarity of the present moment, even when this moment is excruciating. This soft and resolute decision to stay present with what is, opens the door to the power of Now. It gives you the key to a life of clarity, freedom, vibrancy and radiant presence, because this very moment is the only one that is truly alive.

Presence is like a sword of light that cuts through all ghosts of past-fear, and all fantasies of future-hope, to illuminate the stark-naked glory of the life that is unfolding right before your eyes. Presence is a masculine quality because it requires you to pierce the veil of illusion with the laser-beam of your awareness. It is a penetration of the unfoldment of your experience that allows you access to the depth of this moment. It is a shift from a horizontal reality of looking backwards and forwards raggedly, to protect *me* and *mine*, to a vertical reality of deep relaxation within the eternal flow.

It was my resolute willingness to take one step at a time without looking backwards to the past or forwards to the future that allowed the golden staircase in my vision to carry me to my divine destiny. This golden staircase is within you too. It is the guiding light of your truest nature.

This shift from a horizontal perspective to a vertical perspective awakens within you that which is resonant with the true nature of Existence. In this new space, your inner eyes open to see that all separation is an illusion. The gift of laser-beam vision is the revelation of the splendour of oneness. Nothing can withstand the light of truth, least of all the stories of who you think you are. This awakening turns your life around from restlessness to peace, and ends all story-lines of victim-hood.

Presence creates an alignment of the inner power of your Being with the outer power of Creation. And this gives birth to an inner radiance that has the power to re-create your world from the inside out. In the collective vision, this is the emergence of the Golden Child, the divine spark of infinite potential that is expressed through awakened action.

The power of Being is the power of your greatness because you awaken to the truth of your oneness with God. The power of Creation is the power of God's greatness. It is the driving force of all life that goes on and on, re-creating itself anew as the world of form. When the power of Being and the power of Creation come together in alignment, you are reborn as a conscious co-creator of your world. This is a world in which you are no longer a victim of external circumstances, nor even of your own thoughts and feelings. It's a fresh new world in which you can choose how you respond to life.

We are each spiritual beings of infinite magnitude and we have the power to choose what we think, what we feel, what we say and what we do. We have the power to overcome our self-limiting beliefs and to make new choices that affirm our highest potential. We have the power to be all that we dream of and to live our highest potential. We are certainly not victims of life … unless we choose to be.

The resoluteness to be present bestows upon us the power to make new choices. It's a shift from the myopic viewpoint of ego to the 360-degree vision afforded us when we stand in the centre of who we really are. In the fresh vista of vibrant clear-seeing, the world is our oyster and we are the pearl. There is no limit to the ocean of possibility that surrounds us when we are anchored in the truth of our essential nature. The jewel of our Being is forever radiant and waiting to be discovered. All we have to do is look inside.

This essential transformation, from thinking to being, means that our actions are rooted in the power of Presence. When doing arises from our infinite nature it has a very different quality to that of doing as a result of small-minded beliefs. Doing that arises from Being is in harmony with the symphony of the cosmos. Like a divine song, there is a sense of everything being in its rightful place, a perfection that goes way beyond what we may like or dislike. Doing that comes from small-mindedness is out of sync with the bigger picture. There is a dissonance that leads to disharmony.

The power to be rooted in presence, and to know the truth of who you are, is a pivotal point in the journey of becoming an Agent of Change. Without this essential inner transformation our ability to re-create our lives as we wish them to be, and to re-create our world as we wish to see it, would rest on shaky ground. But when change comes from the inside out, there is a congruency between our inner state of consciousness and our outer actions that shoots an arrow of certainty towards our highest destiny. Because this arrow is grounded in our unchanging eternal nature, it taps into the invisible quantum field of infinite potential and calls forth that which is aligned to Divine Plan.

Divine Plan always has the highest good in mind because it arises out of the Mind of God. It is the force of evolution that sees the bigger picture and lifts us out of our smallness into the power of our I AM-ness. It is the creative engine of Existence, the intelligence of life itself. An Agent of Change is aligned to this evolutionary force by always choosing to serve the intelligence and power of I AM.

It is the only way that everlasting positive inner and outer change can happen.

DAILY DECLARATION

Repeat 3 times a day

I choose to rest deeply in the power of this present moment.

I choose, in this moment, to awaken and to know myself as I really AM.

I choose, in this moment, to know myself as a divine creation of infinite potential.

In this moment, I AM whole and I AM holy.

In this moment, I simply AM.

CALL TO ACTION

Your commitment this week is to the application of your awareness as a sword of light. Decide *today* that *wherever* you are and *whatever* you're doing – whether it's washing the dishes, making love or reciting mantras – that you will penetrate each moment with this sword and be present without any stories of liking or disliking. Every time you notice yourself getting caught up in cravings and aversions, wield your sword of light like a samurai warrior – without hesitation, with accuracy and with certainty. A samurai warrior stays resolutely present in the face of pain, horror and even death. And in doing so, he is liberated into greatness … whatever the outcome.

Throughout the day, notice what happens when you're faced with a challenging or painful situation. Do you move away from being present? Do you get caught up in the voices in your head saying '*I'm a failure, I'm weak, I'm not good enough*', or any other self-defeating thought? And do you notice how you lose your power when you identify with these voices?

Each time you notice this is happening, gently but resolutely anchor yourself in that part of you that is deeper and vaster than the voices. Take a moment to feel the wide-open space of your unadulterated I AM-ness. This is the true ground of your being. Each time you move away from the power of Presence simply remind yourself to return to this place. And choose to be rooted here before you take action.

Again, two 5-minute practice sessions are preferable, morning and evening. In these short but intensive periods, apply yourself ruthlessly to the conscious anchoring in the silent space of Being.

SELF-REFLECTION EXERCISE

Reflect back on the events and interactions of your day. Describe in your journal how you responded to each of these. The point here is to become aware of how you respond to challenging situations. Ask yourself if you were fully present. This isn't a contest so you don't have to get it right. What's important is your absolute honesty. Make two lists – the first one for the situations in which you shrank back or turned away, and the second one for the situations in which you were rooted in presence. Make sure you list *all* the situations, both major and minor ... include everything you can recall.

Go through the first list and ask yourself these questions:

✦ How did you feel when you were not fully present? Describe this in detail and include your thoughts, your feelings, and any physical sensations.

✦ What action did you take based on these thoughts and feelings? Be sure to include here your description of not taking any action, if that is what happened.

✦ What was the outcome of this action (or non-action)?

Now go through the second list and ask yourself these questions:

✦ How did you feel when you were fully present? Describe this in detail and include your thoughts, your feelings, and any physical sensations.

✦ What action did you take based on these thoughts and feelings? Be sure to include here your description of not taking any action, if that is what happened.

✦ What was the outcome of this action (or non-action)?

Make sure you don't judge yourself for your responses, simply allow the truth to be revealed.

JOURNAL PAGES

....

....

....

....

....

....

....

....

....

....

....

....

....

....

....

....

....

....

....

....

....

....

....

....

....

....

....

....

....

....

....

....

....

....

....

....

....

....

....

....

....

....

....

....

....

....

TOTALITY
The Power to Love

Totality is saying YES *to Life … and this requires opening wide to welcome everything. Being total means becoming a lover of life … and love is always non-judgmental, inclusive, spacious and all-embracing.*

There's a beautiful quote by the Indian mystic poet Rabindranath Tagore that inspired the title of my first book *How to Find God in Everything*. It says: '*In order to find God, you must welcome everything.*' This touched me to the core when I first read it. The lessons in this chapter and the one that follows, are based on this one simple statement. It's a statement that has profound implications.

Let's start here in Lesson Five with the idea of welcoming everything. How can you possibly open to welcome *everything*? Does this mean welcoming even that which you don't like? Does it mean welcoming even that which hurts? And what about the suffering of the world? This is a question I am asked over and over again.

Your immediate reaction to the idea of opening to welcome everything is likely to be one of feeling over-whelmed. Indeed, the very action – even though it's an *inner* action it's still an action – of opening wide requires a deep relaxation of your consciousness in order to accommodate the vastness of it all. It requires you to go past your comfort zone, but not by overstretching your-self. It's not about straining to achieve something out of your reach. It's about softening and allowing. The will-ingness to simply soften and allow creates a gap in your thinking. And through this aperture, however tiny, you are offered a glimpse of something magnificent.

The truth is, you are far bigger than you *think* you are. Any limits placed on what you can handle are cre-ated by your mind. By this I mean your small mind, the part of you that draws conclusions as to what it can and can't do based on past experience. But this isn't the real you. It's not the total you. Who you really are contains the mind, but is so much more than that. Who you really are has the capacity to hold the totality of life's experience. There is enough space within the real you for all the beauty in the world. There's also enough space for all the ugliness.

Your true nature is love. And love is the bowl of spaciousness that embraces all that is. Love does not deny anyone or anything the milk of human kindness. You do not have to condone unloving actions, but you *can* hold them in tenderness without recoiling in judgment. The power of love is a feminine quality demonstrated by the tenacity to open wide in order to allow in everyone and everything. Sinner or saint, beggar or king … all are welcome in the bosom of the Holy Mother. Love is unfailingly unconditional.

Love is the capacity to simply *be* with an experience. It may be a horrible experience. It may be an excruciating experience. Or even a terrifying experience. But your experience is *as it is* in this moment and no amount of denial will make it any different. Life as it unfolds within your experience *is* happening … and there is nothing you can do about it. No amount of pushing it away and saying it shouldn't be happening will make it go away. Neither will it make you feel any better. The only outcome of fighting against what is, is to shut out love. A reluctant heart is like a creaky door; it moans and groans until a strong wind blows and suddenly it snaps tightly closed leaving you out in the cold. The heart I'm describing here is the emotional heart. It's sensitive and feels deeply, but it cannot bear to be broken open by the pain. The emotional heart is stunted in its capacity for real love. Real love resides in the *spiritual* heart. The spiritual heart is always open and radiant, even when your life – and the world – is falling apart.

There's a well-told story in which a woman, whose only son dies unexpectedly, goes to see an Indian saint. She pleads with him to perform a miracle and bring back her son because she is in such distress. The saint replies: '*I love suffering, it brings me closer to God.*' Suffering, in whatever form it comes, has the capacity to break our hearts wide open. In this breaking, nothing is lost and everything is gained. Heartbreak does not make us less than what we are. On the contrary, we become so much more.

When I say suffering here, I'm not talking about victim-consciousness. This isn't about the egoic suffering expressed as story-lines of 'poor me'. What I'm talking about is the very real suffering experienced when we allow ourselves to feel fully the depth and breadth of our grief. It could be the gut-wrenching sorrow of losing a loved one that leaves you bereft, or a devastating crisis in your finances that takes you to the edge of despair. Or it could be the incredible horror of hearing that thousands of innocent people have died in yet another natural disaster. Whether it's personal or collective suffering that impacts our lives, the willingness to hold the suffering tenderly – without judging it and without trying to change the experience of it – takes us out of our minds and into our hearts.

This is what is meant by Tagore's statement that in order to find God you must welcome everything. In opening to welcome the depth and the breadth of all experience, we are taken to the threshold of Heaven's gate where we can glimpse our true nature in the reflection of God's face. We find God because we fall into the verticality of Being. God has no beginning and no end. And neither do we … when we let go.

Some of us have already had the experience of being catapulted out of the shell of ego into the limitless dimension of Being, and it can be either horribly shocking or pleasantly surprising. The shock comes when your mind scrambles to make sense of it. The surprise comes when you recognize the freedom that comes with letting go. This sudden glimpse of either terrifying or blissful transcendence can be instigated by such activities as peak athletic performance, intense breath-work, childbirth, or the ingestion of psychedelic substances. Whilst this can be a real taste of awakening in which you are filled with an indescribable love, the experience cannot last. Inevitably, disappointment, doubt or even relief will set in. Even more common is the addiction to getting high again, whether this is chemically or spiritually. The problem is, there is no personal evolution in this. And without evolution, there is no real revolution in consciousness.

There is no satisfactory substitute for the power of love that is activated within us when we consciously choose to open; and there is no greater practice than to do so amidst the darkness of our suffering. To softly open your heart amidst the agony is the path of a spiritual warrior. The choice to do this over and over again – even when life crashes down all around you and even when you hate what is going on in the world – is what gives you the power to be an Agent of Change. It is only by having the power to change your inner reality that you are given the power to change your outer reality.

But before you can change anything, your willingness to say *yes* to the experience you are having is crucial. Your experience *is* as it is because it is being experienced. Of course, there's nothing wrong about making decisions that will change your circumstances for the better. But only the *total* acceptance that you are having this experience will lead you to the next step of deciding what to do about it. Without total acceptance, there is only contraction and denial ... and nothing changes.

The invitation is to meet each experience with a

true willingness to be open. In the midst of whatever pain or difficulty you are experiencing, simply notice your resistance. Make a decision, right here and *now*, to stop for a moment and take a deep soft breath. In this momentary gap, make a new choice to meet your experience with friendliness. This impulse of kindness leads to a gentle opening of the heart. It's like a tender embrace that softens the hard edges of your perception. Most often, in the midst of very challenging situations we just don't know *how* to turn our hardness to acceptance. But just being *willing* is enough to bring us closer to the relaxation required for openness and acceptance. Like everything else, it's a practice that gets easier with repetition.

In saying an honest *yes* to the maximum of your capacity in any moment, what unfolds before you offers the potential for deep intimacy. The courage to get right up close to what is, turns you inside out so that you become a naked lover of life. It's a one-to-one relationship in which your senses are open and everything is gloriously vibrant. You see with the awe and innocence of a child. It's a deep acceptance of this moment as it is happening that takes you beyond fear to love. And because you are in love with the process of life, you are deeply nourished by all that is offered within your experience.

Becoming a lover of life has been my spiritual master's gift to me. Before I was graced by Osho's love, I was so cut off from my heart that I was too scared to get close to anyone and certainly too scared to share anything of myself with the world. I was deeply unhappy and I was searching. The gift Osho gave me was to strip me of my defences and blast me into surrender.

In becoming a lover of life, I saw the world through the eyes of the heart. And what I saw changed my reality forever. The heart always sees the perfection in everything – even when things don't go the way we want them to. Perfection means knowing there are no accidents or mistakes in God's plan. When things go wrong or we have bad luck it's because we're blind to the miracle of God's handiwork. There is a greater force orchestrating the whole show behind the scenes, and just because we don't like what we see from our limited ego-perspective doesn't mean it's bad or wrong. The mind rails against what it doesn't understand; the heart trusts the bigger picture even though it cannot be seen in its entirety from where we currently stand.

Having the wisdom to welcome what happens with inner acceptance is a mark of spiritual maturity. Remaining gently open to both the highs and the lows, to both the calamities and the blessings, means you remain unbuffeted by the ebb and flow of life. You become a rock amidst the eddies, an anchor amidst the storm. Just like the farmer in the Zen story, your happiness doesn't depend on the reactivity of small-mind thinking or on the vicissitudes of life.

The inner *yes* aligns you to the power of Creation so that things eventually work in your favour. Life operates on a yes-mechanism only. It's the driving force of all manifestation. It gives rise to all births and to all deaths. It gives rise to all thoughts and to all creations. The process of life could not exist without the power of Yes. It says *yes* to the flowers that bloom and *yes* to the leaves that fall. It says *yes* to every act of genius and *yes* to every act of stupidity. It even says *yes* to suffering.

The power of Creation is the same as the power of the Great Affirmative. Whatever you think, feel, say and do will be met by a *yes*. In other words, whatever you affirm will come back to you. If you say you are a victim – in your thoughts, in your feelings, in your words and in your actions – then life will affirm this. Even a *no* will be met by *yes*. Whatever you have a strong reaction against will be affirmed by life. So rather than making it go away, it will just become even more highlighted. This is how a struggle is set up between what you want and what you get. And even a *yes* that has any tightness around it – because you want it so much you'll be devastated if you don't get it – means that

73

you are unlikely to get what you want. A *yes* that doesn't allow all outcomes has a hidden *no* in it. It is not true acceptance. A true *yes* has no resistance – it is a total surrender. It is wide and open and naked and free. It is unconditional.

It is this unconditionality that works in tandem with the infinite intelligence that guides life. Another name for this intelligence is love. Life simply loves life. That's why it never stops. Life, in some form or another, just keeps on going. Life, just like love, is eternal. It's a perfect self-sustaining plan. That's what the evolutionary process is. By loving whatever appears in your life, you align yourself to this perfection – knowing that every experience that comes your way has been designed especially for your evolutionary growth. Every challenge that forces you to dig deeper into your inner resources and every moment that demands the luminosity of your love is put before you, not because you're being punished by a wrathful God. It's in your life because it's the grit that creates the pearl of your divine destiny. Or as Ram Dass puts it, the 'grist for the mill'.

Perfection is trusting that life loves you *always*, and in *all* ways. Every single thing that exists and every single thing that happens is holy. It is seeded by the Holy Spirit and is gestated in the womb of the Holy Mother. The capacity to see that there is no exception to this gives birth to compassion, both for yourself and for the world. Through the eyes of love you see that all suffering – as well as all joy – is a blessing. Love blesses you and the world with its holiness.

The power to love is more powerful than bullets. It is the only revolution we need because it gives us the strength to re-create the world as we wish to see it. It will be a world built by the wings of angels and by the hearts and hands of humans. A world in which we care for ourselves, for each other, for the planet we live on, and for the whole of Existence.

DAILY DECLARATION

Repeat 3 times daily

I choose to say YES to life and I open wide to welcome everything.

I see through the eyes of my heart and I see perfection in everything.

I AM a lover of life and my love blesses the world with its holiness.

CALL TO ACTION

The decision to say *yes* to life as it unfolds within your experience is a crucial one. This one short word is the driving engine of existence. As you utter this word and as you inhabit its essence and then act from it, you are turbo-charging your inner spiritual muscle into peak performance.

Your task this week is to say *yes* to everything that comes your way. I know this feels scary; what happens if something dangerous arrives at your doorstep or if you are asked to participate in something illicit or harmful? I'm certainly not suggesting you act foolishly. There is a fine line between saying *yes* to something that challenges your comfort zone and saying *yes* to something that is obviously to the detriment of your body, mind and spirit. The *yes* you are being asked to say is initially an embracing of the fact that something has appeared in your life. It is an acceptance of the depth and breadth of feeling you are having around this situation. Only once you have allowed the full *yes*, can you decide on whether to act on it … if action is required, that is.

By the way, if something harmful has appeared in your experience, then it is immensely valuable to ask yourself how come this has entered your life. Perhaps recreational drugs are in your life or an abusive relationship. For many years, alcohol was a feature of my life even though I was not a drinker. My husband at the time loved a few beers most evenings. Often a few beers would turn into an orgy of whiskey and other hard liquor. He kept telling me that I should join in and let my hair down. I kept saying *yes* until I realized that the deeper *yes* I had been avoiding was a *yes* to my feeling that this behaviour was not aligned to my well-being. I finally said *yes* to my truth and *no* to the drinking!

Your self-reflections as you go through the week will be valuable in exploring this issue if it is pertinent to you.

Now that we have highlighted some of the subtleties to this simple exercise, it's time to make the commitment to this week's Call to Action. Decide that you will say a conscious *yes* to whatever happens today. Play with the *yes*, dance with the *yes*. Say *yes* to things that you would normally refuse, as long as they are not harmful. Say *yes* to how you feel, to the highs and lows – celebrate all that life offers you!

Make a big sign in bold bright colours that says '*YES!*' and place it anywhere and everywhere you are likely to see it. Stick it on your desk, on your bathroom mirror, on your car dashboard, write it on your hand … whatever it takes!

SELF-REFLECTION EXERCISE

At the end of each day, describe in your journal your experience of saying *yes* to life's circumstances. Was it easy or difficult? Were you able to do so throughout the day or only at certain times? How did you feel? What was the outcome of your *yes*? Keep writing until you have nothing left to write. This exercise contains layers and layers of insights if you give yourself enough time and space for sacred revelation.

JOURNAL PAGES

....

....

....

....

....

....

....

....

....

....

....

....

....

....

....

....

....

....

....

....

....

....

....

....

....

....

....

....

....

....

....

GRATITUDE
The Power to Receive

Recognize that every experience is a calling from God. God and Life are not separate. God is the process of Life itself. God is all there is.

The power of this lesson lies in the recognition that God does not exist independently of us nor independently of life. God is neither a person nor a thing. Neither is He – or She – some mysterious cosmic entity.

The objectification of God keeps us immature. Even the idea that God does not exist is an objectification. In handing over our internal authority to an external force, we become like helpless children waiting for Our Father to protect us from the pitfalls and hardships of life. This objectification of God is what has happened in all major religious traditions as they have been handed down over the ages.

The belief that God exists on the outside cuts us off from our true source of spirituality. This belief creates a meaningless world in which we are left bereft amidst unbearable suffering. How can we possibly reconcile a world of horrific personal and collective pain with a belief in an omniscient and omnipotent God? Every day thousands of children starve, millions of animals are senselessly slaughtered, and countless people are made homeless or die of sickness. Every day we hear about another war that has erupted, another terrorist attack and another earthquake. How can a supposedly loving God abandon us, His own children? And how can He abandon the world, His own creation?

The answer is, we *can't* make sense of this. And the reason we can't is because we're seeing things incorrectly. We're looking outwardly instead of inwardly. We're searching for salvation from the pain we feel when we perceive an unjust world. We're begging God to answer our prayers for a better life. But the search for salvation is a futile endeavour because it only takes us further away from the only thing that can put a salve on our wound.

The power to heal our suffering lies in our ability to make a revolution in consciousness. This is the decision to stop looking for God outside ourselves, to turn around and to enter the Kingdom of Heaven that lies within. This is a revolution in the sense that we completely change the direction of our focus. And it is revolutionary in the sense that it is radical. It challenges the status quo of our own conditioning and it questions the tradition of conventional religion.

The bare truth is – God is not something you can search for. God is what happens when you drop the search. It's what happens when you rest so deeply within your Being-nature that all separation between inner and outer dissolves. It's what happens when you realize – or you come to see with your real eyes – that the glory of Divine Oneness expresses itself through everything.

GOD is the Grand Omnipresent Designer. God is not only the mastermind of Existence but also the ever-present and ever-unfolding expression of all that exists. He is both the architect and the architecture. God *is* every human being, every living creature, every blade of grass and every grain of dust. God *is* every galaxy, every star, every supernova, every black hole and every atom. God *is* everything we create, every event, every action, every thought, every feeling and every breath. There is no thing that is not God. God is Life ... and the *process* of Life itself.

The spiritual maturity required to see that God is

all there is, allows us to drop the search ... once and for all. Dropping the search entails the recognition that everything – *without exception* – is a calling from God. Everything that unfolds within your life, whether blissful or terrible, has been called forth from within yourself as a way to experience the divinity that resides within you *as* you. There is such a deep inner relaxation when we finally see that everything is an expression of the Divine, when we finally recognize that everything is sacred. And there is such liberation when we finally have the cellular remembrance that this sacredness is indivisible from our own true nature.

Dropping the search does not mean giving up. It is not a surrender to the enemy, for there is no enemy. It is simply – and profoundly – a surrender of ego's incessant search for something outside itself to make things better, bigger, stronger, safer. It is a complete halt of ego's race into the future to bring something back into the present in order to fix it. As we stop this race, we end the insanity that is the root cause of all suffering in ourselves and in the world. We come to a standstill in which we rest unencumbered in the unfoldment of now.

This kind of surrender is a sign of strength in which we grow in spiritual stature. We rise above the childish superstition of praying for our wishes to be granted and we enter a new dimension in which we 'ask and it is given'. Jesus said this very same thing in the Sermon on the Mount: '*All things whatsoever ye pray and ask for, believe that ye have received them, and ye shall receive them.*' This statement is so easy to misunderstand when we're standing in the sidelines of our smallness. From ego's point of view, it means pleading for what we think we need in order to feel better, safer, richer, stronger, happier … or whatever else is on our list. But Jesus stood in the blazing glory of his greatness when he spoke these words. What he meant was that we should not wait for good things to happen in order to feel grateful, but instead we should choose to feel grateful – whatever our circumstances – and then good things will come to us.

I know how incredibly difficult it is to be grateful during hard times. How can you be grateful for the loss of a loved one, the loss of a job, or the loss of your home? I've been there; I've experienced every single one of these and more. And it's especially difficult to be grateful amidst the crazy times we live in. How can you be grateful for the greed, the corruption and the terror that trickle down from global arenas of politics, economics and profit-based commerce?

Even though it severely challenges us to be grateful for the things we don't want or like, let alone the things that hurt us, it really doesn't serve us to shrink back and hide at times like these. Neither does it serve us to harden into a tight ball of rage. The resistance we embody when we try to avoid or fight what hurts us, only serves to add to the negativity. A wiser approach is to actively choose to embrace the suffering.

The power of gratitude lies in the fact that it is a conscious choice; it is a *cause* not an effect. Digging deep to find gratitude for even those things that we would rather cast out from our lives sends an arrow of love right into the heart of darkness. It's far more powerful than denial or hate. This arrow has the power to set aglow both your inner world and your outer world so that you can see clearly through the eyes of holiness. And with this unobstructed vision you are welcomed into the abiding peace of an unbounded heart.

Gratitude melts the hard knot of fear that prevents you from resting in the truth of who you are. And it dissolves the mental projections that lead you to believe in a fearful world. In healing the split between good and bad, gratitude has the power to awaken you to the truth that there ultimately is no evil. There are only the shadows created by your own unilluminated thoughts.

Gratitude is like making a decision to draw back the curtains and let the sun's rays enter a darkened room. Gratitude is the cause; awakening is the effect.

Making a conscious choice to be grateful when your

life is rocked by an unwelcome event, opens your heart so that you can receive the goodness – and the God-ness – available to you beneath the details of your story. Whether it's a personal story of unexpected illness, divorce or bankruptcy, or a global story of catastrophic famine, flooding or financial collapse, it's in your field of perception for a reason. It's here so that you can overcome your small-minded perspective and choose the heavenly radiance of love over the hellish stark-ness of fear.

Love is more effective in transforming your life and the world than fear because God does not respond to begging for salvation but to a heart full of gratitude for what's already here. The power of Creation and the power of God can only be accessed right here in the present, not at some time in the future. Only the present is real, so reality can only be created in the here and now. It's not about wishing for more money, more success, more romance or more anything, because that's focusing on a future moment that does not yet exist. It's about changing your vibrational frequency right *now* so that you inhabit that which you wish to be.

What all this is really saying is, don't focus on what's wrong or what's missing but instead turn your attention to the ever-present fullness beneath your story-lines. If you want to experience more prosperity and abundance in your life, choose to inhabit the richness that is already here within the radiant jewel of your essential nature; this is the you that is without stories of not having enough. If you want to experience more recognition and success in your life, choose to embody the fulfilment that is already here in the core of your true self: this is the you that is untarnished by stories of not being enough. And if you want to experience more love and completeness in your life, choose to reside in the wholeness of love that is already here in every atom of your being; this is the you that is without stories of not being loved enough.

When we dig deep, we realize that the things we always want more of – money, success, relationships – are really the physical manifestation of the spiritual qualities of the heart. By going directly to the source for what we want, right *here* in our hearts, we open the door to a world of miracles. Gratitude is the key.

In the collective vision, it was one tiny moment of gratitude that changed everything. In my darkest hour, as I was about to die, I mustered a grain of true gratitude for the totality of my truncated life. This grain contained all I had received so far, both the good and the bad. It was in this very moment that the flame of awakening was lit in the centre of my heart. From this moment on, my world was never the same as before.

The embrace of what's already here within the bowl of your heart makes you receptive. Each of us has a divine blueprint, an energetic matrix waiting to be downloaded from the unmanifest dimension into the world of form. The only thing that stands in the way is you. Or more accurately, your story-lines of 'poor me' that lead to resistance and struggle. Receptivity is the resolve to meet these story-lines, and the ensuing layers of pain, blame and shame, with gentle but unwavering awareness; but not to stop there. Receptivity involves the willingness to dive into the spaciousness that is ever present beneath and beyond everything you tell yourself is stopping you from living your greatness.

What God is waiting for is the declaration of your readiness to receive. So pray not for what you want, but pray that you are made available. Your honest availability opens up your inner knowing so that you see, hear and feel the details of your divine blueprint. Just like the steps of the golden staircase that unfolded before my eyes one at a time, all you are required to do is to begin the journey by taking one step at a time.

The power to receive allows the mystery of life to unfold with perfect grace. Grace is an inexplicable sense of flow that cannot be grasped by the mind. It can only be experienced in the depth of our Being-ness. It is grace that allows the possibility of personal and global transformation. Our job is to prepare the way ... the rest is up to God. The more diligently we clear the ground we stand on from the debris of ego's wanting, the more abundance, fulfilment and love will be available to us. Not only do our wildest dreams then have the possibility of coming true, but the dream of a better world has a chance of becoming a reality.

A world in which each individual is fulfilled in belly, heart and soul is a world in which voracious greed, ambition and self-gratification will lose their allure. It's a world in which feathering one's own nest will be replaced by caring and sharing ... because there really is enough for all. And it's a world in which profit at all costs will be replaced by a win-win situation for the benefit of all ... because we can climb to greater heights when we're all on the same side. It's a new world in which the spiritual and the material come together.

DAILY DECLARATION

Repeat 3 times daily

Gratitude is a conscious choice I make in every moment.

I choose to see everything as a gift from the Divine.

I AM available for all that is good in my life.

I AM available for all that is God in my life.

CALL TO ACTION

This lesson is not too dissimilar from the previous one. Your task here is to choose to be grateful for everything that happens in your life; to consciously accept the good, the bad and the ugly as gifts from God. This is powerful stuff. Undoubtedly you will recoil when something challenges your capacity for gratitude. In these moments, take a pause. Breathe and soften into the experience. Say *yes* to it and dive beneath what you don't like. Know that there is a hidden gift in everything. And if you really can't access the gratitude that resides in the depths of your spiritual heart, then simply say:

Dear God, Even though I cannot see what is good or godly about this painful/challenging situation, I am willing to embrace it and to be grateful for the gifts that are currently hidden from me. May I open my eyes to that which I cannot see from where I now stand. And may I receive all that is good and all that is God.

Remember that this is a process of self-inquiry. You are bringing the light to the dark and this is sometimes difficult as there is a deep cleansing of all that stands in the way of love. You may not like what is revealed and you may be resistant to continuing the journey. Be kind to yourself; remember that you are exercising a spiritual muscle that has perhaps been neglected for a long time. Practice makes perfect.

Practise the power of gratitude as often as you remember throughout the day.

SELF-REFLECTION EXERCISE

At the end of the day, preferably just before you go to sleep, review your day in your mind's eye and feel gratitude for every single thing that happened, even if it was unpleasant, difficult or painful, and even if you could not do so at the time. Be grateful for the deeper gift inside the experience, even if you cannot see what that is right now. Allow your words to flow freely onto the pages of your journal until you feel complete. And then let it go … and sleep sweetly.

JOURNAL PAGES

....

....

....

....

....

....

....

....

....

....

....

....

....

....

....

....

....

....

....

....

....

....

....

....

....

....

....

....

FORGIVENESS
The Power to Heal

Recognize that everyone and everything is a manifestation of God. Every single person and every single thing that exists originates from the same Source. We are all manifestations of the One Consciousness That Is All … even that which appears – to our minds – to be not so.

If you're on a spiritual path, then most likely you've been touched by the Divine, expressing itself through something beautiful. It's that sense of the intangible, the ineffable and the uncontainable that leads to wonder and awe. Perhaps you've felt it whilst looking up at the infinity of a starry sky or whilst watching the miracle of sunrise over the horizon. Perhaps you've felt it whilst gazing into the timeless innocence of a child's eyes, or dancing wildly until you disappear into a whirlwind of ecstasy. Or just sitting still in the eternity of deep silence. Whether you call this kind of experience God, the Source, or Oneness, the overriding impression is of coming home to rest in wholeness.

But what happens when you're faced with something ugly? Or something cruel? There's nothing inherently wrong with feeling the horror of ugliness or cruelty. Certainly, it's uncomfortable and we recoil. But that's about all there is to it. The real problem starts when our mind interprets it as bad or wrong. Or even evil. The perception of bad, wrong or evil leads to a deep inner rage. It's a primal rage at the womb of Creation, the Great Mother, for depriving us of goodness. This has its roots in preverbal infancy when the breast – our only source of nourishment – is made unavailable. This unavailability may have been unavoidable, as in the case of a mother who is sick and cannot nurse her child. Or it may have been due to misguided child-rearing practices, as in the case of putting a baby on the bottle before it is ready. Or it may have been more sinister than that, as in the case of a mother who unconsciously resents breast-feeding and ignores the cry of a hungry infant. Whatever the reason, we interpret this unavailability of the source of our survival as denial of love.

And so we experience the dark face of the mother for the first time. In our eyes, she becomes bad.

Because, at such an early stage of our development, our mother is our world, our rage becomes a rage at the world for not being good, and for not being God. And so the primordial oneness of our prebirth consciousness ruptures and we separate from our own essential God-ness. It's an archetypal wound that is mythologized by the expulsion from the Garden of Eden and is imprinted in our psyches as Original Sin. It's the innate shame of being not good enough or perfect enough to receive God's love.

This archaic belief has serious repercussions on our lives. It blinds us to the truth of how things really are. When something hurts so much we cannot bear it, we attempt to get rid of it by projecting it onto something outside of ourselves. This projection of our woundedness means we see others and the world as not good enough or as imperfect; this results in the mental distortion of resentment, blame and hate. The alternative projection of our woundedness inwards means we see ourselves as not good enough or as imperfect; this results in the mental distortion of guilt, shame and unworthiness. If the wound is buried inside long enough, it becomes an emotional distortion such as depression, anxiety, or even psychosis. And eventually it can become a physical distortion in the form of cancer, arthritis or any other severe illness. All mental, emotional and physical dis-ease is an effect of our own distorted perceptions.

Collectively, this has a huge impact. Six billion individuals, split off from their own essential goodness and their essential God-ness, creates a world of division. The war, violence and poverty we see in the world are a reflection of our own warring, violent and impoverished thoughts and feelings. The more we judge, hate and resist what we perceive as bad, wrong or evil, the more we attract judgment, hate and resistance into our lives. And so the cycle is perpetuated to create our current reality.

We do not heal the world by fighting it but by embracing it as it is. The darkness we perceive is only a reflection of where we have failed to illuminate the world with our love.

If we truly want to re-create the world as Heaven on Earth, we need to practise seeing God in everyone and everything. It's a practice because it's excruciatingly difficult to see divinity in the dirt. It's so much easier to walk around with our heads in the clouds looking at only the pretty things. But the bottom line is, we can't decide to just see divinity where we want to see it and expect to live a life of peace. A peaceful world can only arise when we are each at peace with ourselves. And this means being at peace with how things are.

This is the practice of forgiveness. Many people have great difficulty with the idea – let alone with the practice – of forgiveness because they think it's about turning the other cheek and allowing themselves to be abused. But forgiveness is not forgetting. It's not about pretending to be not hurt when really you have been. It's not about ignoring the suffering, either your own or someone else's. And it's certainly not about being a victim. It's far deeper than any of that.

Forgiveness is a radical shift in perception in which you choose to see through the rise and fall of drama to the underlying ground of Being from which all forms are born and into which all forms die. This penetrating insight gives us the power to see through unconscious actions to the purity of essence at the core of each human being. This is what is meant by Jesus' statement as he lay on the cross waiting to die: '*Forgive them Father, for they know not what they do.*' It's the ultimate sacrifice – the sacrifice of the ego on the altar of God. But it's a sacrifice that makes us greater, not less, than all that we think we are.

What this means in everyday terms is that whilst we are not required to condone the hurtful acts of others, it's to our benefit not to hold onto blame, resentment and revenge. Our greatest power in the face of what hurts lies in our willingness to acknowledge the pain and then to move on. Forgiveness cannot right a wrong, but it can make whole that tender place in your heart that was torn asunder. The power of forgiveness lies in the return to love.

As in the collective vision, the willingness to let go of our story-line of how *'this shouldn't be happening to me'* allows the milk of human kindness to flow once again. Forgiveness has the power to mend everything that was broken mentally, emotionally and physically. In releasing those that we condemn as wrong, bad or evil from the bondage of our own judgment, we release ourselves from the tyranny of our distorted perceptions.

In the face of incredible injustice and cruelty, we are called upon to be compassionate enough to forgive that which appears – to our minds – to be the opposite of love. It's the only way to heal our wounds. And it's our only hope of salvation.

There are many extraordinary stories of people from all walks of life who have been in terrible situations, such as captivity and torture, and who have transcended their victim-consciousness by forgiving their persecutors and developing a depth and breadth of compassion that has only served to enhance their power not diminish it. Many of these have gone on to offer something of lasting value to the world. And many of them have become leading lights in the political, social and spiritual arenas.

Think of Nelson Mandela who has progressed from 30 years' captivity as a political prisoner to become President of South Africa, a Nobel Prize winner and a key player in the dismantling of apartheid. Think of the Dalai Lama who had to flee his country, in exile in the face of horrific cruelty to his people and has become a powerful voice for a compassionate world. And think of some of the Holocaust victims who inspire us to greater heights of humanity by their capacity to forgive inhuman acts. More recently I have been moved by news of a young man in the USA who was wrongly accused of rape and incarcerated for life. He chose to forgive the woman who was responsible for the error and their ensuing friendship led to his release. Today they work together as a powerful team to focus awareness on accurate crime identification.

Each one of these stories – and there are hundreds more if we take the time to look – is another beacon that guides us through the valley of darkness and shows us what it is to be truly human.

What can be overlooked in all of this is that grief is very often a part of the journey of forgiveness. And this is what we try to avoid, for grief is a descent into the underworld of our own unresolved thoughts and feelings. To the ego this is a threat. To the heart it is a blessed relief. Beneath the stony resistance there is a torrent of tears waiting to flood through our consciousness and wash away our pain. I have seen this happen quite literally with my husband who suffered from a major illness for several years. His journey of healing took him through an emotional cleansing that ended up at forgiveness, and a total transformation to radiant health.

When you stop putting up barriers to love – whether this be self-love, love of others or love of the world – original sin is erased and the wound of separation is healed. Forgiveness is your natural state. It is a return to wholeness; a return to holiness. In the eyes of holiness, there is only holiness, which recognizes that everyone and everything is a manifestation of God. The power to transform your inner and outer reality lies within this lesson.

Once again, it is a practice. It's a spiritual muscle that gets stronger the more you use it. Even though it feels like an effort to make this shift in perception, it does get easier the more you exercise it. At some point in the practice you will undoubtedly forgive yourself for your erroneous thinking and you will wonder how you could ever have seen anything as unholy!

I invite you, right here and *now*, to make a decision to take 100 per cent responsibility for how you perceive things. There's no use waiting for someone else to make your life or the world a better place. And there's certainly no point waiting for some time in the future when you feel like being compassionate. Only *you* can decide to forgive. The power to choose to see, think and feel through the eyes of love is the most important contribution you can make to *your* life ... and to *all* of life.

DAILY DECLARATION

Repeat 3 times daily

I choose to know that all forms are born from Divine Mind.

I choose to see the light of God in everyone and in everything.

I AM whole and I AM holy ... I see the world through the eyes of holiness.

CALL TO ACTION

When asked how she was able to go amongst the lepers to hold them and tend to their wounds, Mother Teresa said: '*Each one of them is Jesus in disguise.*' This week

CHANGE YOUR LIFE, CHANGE YOUR WORLD

you are called to act like a saint. By this I do not mean that you have to do charitable things, but that you see through the eyes of holiness.

Start your day by saying to yourself: '*Today I choose to recognize that everyone and everything is a manifestation of God*'. As you go about your day and interact with your world, say out loud or internally: '*You are God*'. Or, if you prefer: '*You are the Divine*'. Say this every time you meet a person or even walk past a stranger on the street. Say this every time you notice a tree, flower, animal or even the sky. And say this every time you have a powerful emotion, feeling or thought. Each time you say '*You are God*' or '*You are the Divine*', imagine the centre of your chest opening and allow the essence of the person or thing you are interacting with to enter the temple of your heart. Notice, as you go about your day, how easy or difficult this is. Perhaps you will find that all struggle dissolves and you are left basking in a feeling of oneness. Make a special note of this!

Spend a few minutes at the end of the day, just before you go to sleep, holding in your mind anyone you judge, resent, envy, dislike or hate. Breathe softly and deeply ... and allow them to enter the temple of your heart. Give yourself permission, just for now at least, to see through their unconscious actions that may have harmed you or another. See through to the purity of their heart and recognize them as a manifestation of the Divine. Practise this for as long as necessary, until you feel a sense of peace. Now let this practice go ... and sleep sweetly.

SELF-REFLECTION EXERCISE

At the end of the day, before your bed-time practice, write in your journal. Describe your thoughts and feelings as you went about your day practising seeing the Divine in everyone and in everything. Were there some people and some things that were easier than others? Let your insights flow.

JOURNAL PAGES

....

....

....

....

....

....

....

....

....

....

....

....

....

....

....

....

....

....

....

....

....

....

....

....

....

....

....

....

....

....

NAKEDNESS
The Power to Trust

Be naked as a baby ... in other words, have the
courage to bare yourself to the world and to God.

We come into this world naked; both literally and meta-phorically. With eyes wide and belly soft, we meet the world in open innocence. We're vulnerable, but this vulnerability does not hinder us. We haven't yet learnt to defend ourselves from what hurts.

Look into a child's eyes and you will see a fierce open-ness. I say fierce because this openness is unrelenting. It does not waver at what you might call bad and it does not turn away at what you might call ugly; everything is worthy of its gaze. This naked awareness simply sees things as they are, not as you might label them to be.

Just as in God's eyes, there is nothing higher or lower, no better or worse; everything is created equal.

But as time goes on, we learn that some things hurt. And we learn that some things hurt more than others. At some stage, we decide we don't want to be hurt again. This is especially so in the arena of intimate relationships. When it comes to significant people in our lives – parents, siblings, close friends, lovers, spouses – we attempt to avoid hurt at all costs. We want love to look – and to feel – a certain way. And if it doesn't come in the form we expect or like then we decide it is not love after all.

This decision has massive ramifications. It means we invest our energy in turning away from the fullness of this moment. We stop trusting that what is being offered here in this experience – and in *every* experience – is nothing other than love itself. This lack of willingness to remain fiercely open in the face of everything means we attempt to insulate ourselves from what we imagine will hurt us. The insulation takes the form of our favourite story-lines – the things we tell ourselves in order to avoid the full depth of our feelings. Whatever the story and however justified we might feel about it, the effect is detrimental to our lives. Whether we believe that it's our parent's fault for messing us up, or whether we believe our lover is to blame for that ache in our heart, the avoidance of what hurts takes attention away from the aliveness of what is present and ultimately saps our life-force.

Look into the eyes of an ageing person and, unless they live an awakened life, you will see that the transparency of original innocence has been lost. It's as if a veil has been drawn to keep out the world. This closing down is inevitable if we identify with who we *think* we are. But, who we think we are is built on rocky foundations. It is based on the story of 'personality'. And that's exactly what it is – a story. It is the story put together by your familial, educational, social and cultural conditioning. Before you were born, this story did not exist. And when you die, the story will fade away. But who you *really* are – the open bowl of consciousness within which all stories appear and disappear – has always been here. And always will be.

When we give our attention to that which is not true, we have no choice but to defend this at all costs. The survival of the ego depends on it. The ego relies on getting love in the form of approval, status, emotional gratification … anything and everything that makes it feel special or 'better than'. The fear of annihilation when this erroneous identity is exposed is a devastating blow to the ego's unstable structure. And so we put all our effort into hardening and hiding. We fortify the fragile shell of ego with the roles we play. We identify with '*I am a dedicated mother*' or '*I am a successful entrepreneur*' or '*I am a free-spirited artist*'; or even '*I am an evolved spiritual being*'. Every part of ourselves that we deem not worthy of being seen, we throw behind this façade. Usually this is the opposite of what we have identified with. It's what we label bad or wrong or ugly. Maybe it's that part of us which is selfish, lazy or flaky; or even unspiritual. Robert Bly calls this the 'shadow bag'. The problem is that along with what we don't want or don't like, we also throw away the only thing that is truly alive – the inner flame of our naked innocence. And without this radiance to light our path, we stop trusting life and we stop trusting love.

This is what you see when you look into the eyes of a person who has succumbed to fear. You see someone who has stopped living authentically because they do not have the courage to embrace the good, the bad and the ugly within themselves. And you see someone who has stopped relating authentically because they do not dare to bare themselves, warts and all. It's one of life's paradoxes that not only do we fear that our darkness will be rejected, but we also fear that our light will be stolen. Without the willingness to let both the dark and the light be seen, true relationship – to ourselves, to each other, to the world and to life – is impossible. This is the sense of alienation so many people experience. It is a self-imposed amputation from innate wholeness.

For many people this alienation goes on to the end of their life. Death becomes the final opportunity for awakening in which they are offered the recognition of their essential oneness. But for some, there comes a time when the suffering created by the inner separation is no longer a viable option; it's just too great a burden to bear. For these people, there is a wake-up call. It could be a personal calamity that arrives on their doorstep, such as sudden illness or the death of a beloved or bankruptcy; or all of these all at once. It could be a glimpse of oneness afforded by a transcendent experience through meditation, primal therapy or psychedelics, that then leads to an emotional breakdown – or breakthrough – as everything once held to be true falls apart. If you're serious about the desire to discover the truth, then the calamity becomes a portal to awakening.

The resolve to live and to love authentically engages us on the return journey to innocence. It's an unravelling of ego's defences that brings us home to original nakedness. It's a journey that requires the willingness to be hurt, to face the fear and to see honestly what lies beneath. The revelation of what lies beneath any feeling or any experience is that which is always present and can never be hurt. Within the depths of what you perceive as darkness lies a treasure waiting to be discovered. In tenderly embracing what you'd rather keep in the shadows, the jewel of your radiant nature is revealed. It is the divine light of love at the core of everything.

In naked awareness, you see that love is always here, whatever form it may take. Love has always been here; it is only you who has been too blind to see. Both your greatest friend and your greatest enemy are here to awaken your capacity to love. My greatest teacher has been my mother. Our relationship has been an incredibly challenging one to me, and for most of my adult life I was adamant that she was the cause of my pain. But the defences I created to keep her out of my heart only served to keep the real me locked up inside. It's only when I gathered the resolve to strip myself of my story-lines of victim-hood that I saw that she was an angel in disguise. This recognition has given me the power to be myself and to make new choices. Approaching my mid-life cycle, I am still deeply challenged by having to meet my own unilluminated thoughts about my mother. But it's an on-going journey I'm prepared to take because it has released within me a deeper compassion for all who suffer.

Your true power is born out of the courage to be naked. In the willingness to be vulnerable, you are shown that which is invulnerable. This invulnerability is a transparency. It means nothing has a hold on you. It simply passes through because you do not react unconsciously, but instead choose to stand in the light of awareness. There is truly nothing that can hurt you ... only what your mind judges as evil. Nakedness gives you the power to trust. It gives you the power to know that you are good. And to know that you are God. It does not serve you nor does it serve the world to keep the light of your God-ness hidden. It is your authentic self.

What the world needs most of all is not your achievements or your accolades. Neither does it need your righteousness. What the world needs most of all is your authenticity. Authenticity gives you the capacity to relate. Authentic relating consists of two hearts meeting, not two egos clashing. The heart can speak and hear truth – the ego cannot. Taking full responsibility for how you feel shifts you from the blame-game to real communication; and it's only real communication that leads to a resolution of conflict.

Imagine a world built on authentic relationships. Imagine men and women, families and friends, work colleagues and business partners coming together in nakedness; in other words, without personal agenda. Such a coming together between individuals, between groups and even between nations would give rise to co-creative partnerships in which the highest possible outcome for all is the only goal. Imagine the new solutions to old problems that would become available to us in the spirit of collaboration.

There is enough money, enough food, and enough love for every single person on this planet. What will make this available to everyone is the shift from a *me*-centred to a *we*-centred relationship to life. As each of us awakens to the truth of who we are, so we will begin to see that we are all connected much more intimately than we had ever imagined. Rather than bind us to each other, the awareness of our interconnectedness frees us from the skin-encapsulated ego and leads to a convergence of hearts in which we surf on a collective wave to a new harmonic world.

This radically new way of being heralds the dawn of a bright future in which the light of God prevails on Earth.

DAILY DECLARATION

Repeat 3 times daily

I choose to live in the wonder of now.

I choose to experience every moment as an adventure to be met with eyes wide open and belly soft.

I AM at one with God … because God is with me wherever I go.

CALL TO ACTION

The lesson this week is to imagine yourself to be transparent. As you go about your daily interactions, allow everything that happens to just pass through you. Imagine your body, your mind and your heart are all transparent as you speak to people, as you eat your meals, as you sit at your computer, as you go to work, as you walk and as you breathe. It's not something that can be implemented by the thinking mind. It is an energetic transparency that is understood by the soul. But it also helps to imagine your physical body – your skin, your eyes, your liver, your lungs and all other organs – as transparent.

Each time you notice a slight retraction into a familiar defence pattern, simply take a pause and breathe softly and deeply. Imagine the defence melting and allow yourself to be naked. Allow all conversations, all transactions, all that you touch and all that you see to flow right through you.

This transparency leads not only to an unfathomable trust in life, but also to the awakening of your own translucent nature. Not only are you able to receive more light, but you are also able to transmit more light. And so you are able to walk more lightly through your life.

SELF-REFLECTION EXERCISE

At the end of each day, reflect on all your interactions and write in your journal. Describe your experience of being naked by answering these questions:

✦ Did you notice any defences that you used to protect yourself from feeling uncomfortable or being hurt? Were these mental defences, such as thoughts of judgment or blame? Or emotional defences, such as numbing out or getting angry? Or physical defences, such as feeling lethargic or hyperactive? Defences are any way of relating to life that leads to a moving away from what is happening.

✦ What did you do to dissolve these defences? Did you breathe? Did you soften the tension in your body? Did you change your thoughts? Perhaps you visualized your body becoming transparent?

✦ How did you feel when you became transparent?

✦ What was the outcome of the interaction when you allowed yourself to become transparent?

Write freely without censoring. Remember that what is important here is your honesty. Practise authentic relating to yourself. And remember that this exercise may be a little challenging at first … but that practice makes perfect!

JOURNAL PAGES

....

....

....

....

....

....

....

....

....

....

....

....

....

....

....

....

....

....

....

....

....

....

....

....

....

....

....

....

....

....

....

....

....

....

....

....

SERVICE
The Power to Give

In every moment you have the choice to serve ego or to serve God – the former impoverishes you, the latter enriches you.

In every moment you stand at a crossroads where you are asked to make the most important choice you have ever been faced with. In every moment you can choose to serve ego or you can choose to serve God. The decision you make has the power to fundamentally change the direction of your life. It is the absolute key to your empowerment.

All the previous lessons have been building up towards this one. Up until now you've been polishing the jewel of your radiant nature so that you can finally ask yourself which direction you will choose. It's taken up until now to prepare yourself because the question needs to arise from within you. In asking the question you demonstrate that you have developed an inner spiritual muscle that gives you the power to re-create your inner and outer world.

The shift from serving ego to serving God sounds like an esoteric path but it's actually a decision that turns you towards the world, not away from it. The whole point of developing an inner spiritual muscle is to serve the world by activating your capacity to be an Agent of Change. It is the key to a new you and to a new world.

The new evolutionary impulse coming through humanity today demands that we make the transition from taking to giving. It's a shift from self-gratification to service that lifts us out of ego and into our highest destiny. It is the fulfilment of our highest destiny that will fast-forward our personal as well as our planetary evolution.

The time for moving out of an archaic survival mode has come. Even though we live amidst dramatic times in which our personal and planetary survival has become an issue, we are being called to see through the illusion of helplessness that this engenders. We are being called to a new way of being, in which we choose love over fear. Because it is love that will change the world.

Our old habitual way of seeing things and of doing things is based on erroneous thinking. The ego looks outside itself for fulfilment because its primary belief is in scarcity. In believing itself to be not good enough, not rich enough, not happy enough, not beautiful enough, not powerful enough – or any other adjective you wish to name, the list is endless – it always wants more. And in believing there is not enough money, happiness, beauty or power in the world, it wants more as quickly as possible lest someone else gets to it first. Ego's primary motivation is self-serving gain. And so it seeks to get as much as it can from people, from the world and from life. It even prays to God to get its wishes granted. On a global level, it has led to a world of insatiable greed and blinkered competitiveness in which the effect on our humanity, on our world and on our planet is disregarded.

This way of seeing things is the path of fear. It inevitably leads to separation, and it creates a vicious cycle of wanting more. The voracious appetite for immediate gratification is what leads to all addictive behaviours, including addictions to food, to intoxication, to romantic love, to money, to possessions and to power. But far from empowering us, this approach to life only serves to diminish us. The overriding compulsion to getting what you think you need in order to feel better about yourself is a limitation. It keeps you within the confines of a comfort zone in which you're running away from what scares you and running towards what gratifies you. There is no growth in this.

It's only in having the courage to take a step beyond what makes you feel safe and secure that you grow wings and learn to fly. The bottom line is that the ego is not what it pretends to be. For all its pomp and posturing, it is in fact a coward. It would rather live in the hope of salvation than take the leap into freedom right here and now. I invite you to examine your belief system for any traces of the 'one day syndrome'. Do you believe that one day you will be rich, that one day you will be happy, that one day you will find the perfect partner, or that one day you will discover your true purpose? And do you believe that one day you will be enlightened? I invite you to inquire honestly … are you willing to let go of all these dreams? In *this* moment, are you willing to be free?

The willingness to stretch the boundaries of your comfort zone is an act of daring. It's a sacrifice that demands the willingness to stand at the edge of the precipice and let yourself fall into the abyss of the unknown. What the ego doesn't know is that it won't actually die – it will be reborn. The very act, metaphorically, of jumping into the abyss with the willingness to die is what transforms the ego from being a tyrant who runs the whole show to its rightful role as a servant.

This transformation is a shift in consciousness that changes everything. And it's the whole point of the evolutionary wave that is washing through humanity today. It's the shift from being motivated by self-service to being motivated by being of service. A brand new you and a brand new world come into existence when you are less motivated by self-serving gain and immediate gratification, and more motivated by making a contribution to the bigger picture. Being of service is the desire to offer your unique brilliance to the world so that you not only enrich your own life but also the lives of others. It's not just about doing good things or about being a good person. It's not even about holding hands and praying for world peace. It's about knowing that what we do for others we also do for the benefit of ourselves. It's a higher perspective in which we see that our actions, our words and our thoughts have a long-range effect on everything that exists.

Ultimately, it's about making the choice in *every* moment – *whatever* you're doing – to open rather than close. It's about choosing – even when things appear difficult – the grandeur of open-heartedness over the petty concerns of self-centredness. It's that part of you that says *yes* to life and enables you to bring your totality – in other words, the full depth of your presence and the full breadth of your openness – into the unfoldment of each moment.

The evolutionary call is that we inhabit the fullness of our inner radiance and bring forth our greatness. Your greatness is your highest destiny. It means being all that you truly are so that you play your rightful role within Divine Plan. It means being at the leading edge of your life, the place just outside your comfort zone where you're called to give your excellence to your relationships, to your work, to your health, to your community and to your planet. The leading edge is where you choose to take responsibility for optimal physical, emotional, mental, spiritual and environmental well-being so that you live a life of radiance. For it's only in living a radiant life that you can truly be of service.

We each have a divine mission, something we are here to fulfil whilst incarnated in an earthly body. The shape or form does not matter, for there is no job description that is higher or lower in God's eyes. In fact, your job is the same as mine – to be a servant of God. And this could take the form of spiritual teacher, salesperson, single mother … or any other role we can name. What matters is what we bring to this role. We each have a ministry, a community that we are here to serve whilst we inhabit earthly bodies. This could be a ministry made up of just one person or it could be made up of 100 or 1,000 people. It could even be a ministry of one million. But this should not be our concern; this is a matter for God to take care of. There's a great humility that comes with daring to step into the leading edge of your life and then letting go of the details.

Your real job – like mine and like everyone else's – is to go inside and awaken in order to serve the world with the fragrance of your essential love-nature. When *doing* is rooted in the essence of *being* then real change can happen. It's called awakened action, and it's the pinnacle of becoming an Agent of Change. Awakened action accelerates you into a new paradigm of unity in which whatever serves the world also serves you. It's a win-win situation in which true fulfilment becomes available to each and every one of us. The capacity to offer our awakening through everything that we do brings us into alignment with the co-creative evolutionary frequency of our times.

It's the birth of a new human being; and it's where we're headed as a species.

DAILY DECLARATION

Repeat 3 times daily

I choose to serve God by making myself available
for the download of my Divine Mission.

I AM here to shine the light of my magnificence
on everything I say and do.

I AM here to know the truth of my infinite
potential.

I AM here to remember my divinity and to
manifest my destiny.

CALL TO ACTION

The journey you have been on so far is reaching its
climax. You have dug deep to unearth the weeds in
the garden of your consciousness. You have shone a
light where there was darkness to reveal the treasure
at your core. And you have polished the facets of your
diamond-nature so that your inner radiance becomes
the constancy in your life. Now it's time to ask the
questions that hold the potential to launch you to a new
level of personal evolution.

But before you do that, you need to make yourself available for this acceleration. Each morning, take

at least 5–10 minutes of silence. You may like to light a candle and burn some incense. Enter the inner sanctuary of your heart by breathing softly with your attention on the centre of your chest as it rises and falls. When your mind is quiet and your body is relaxed, imagine the crown of your head opening and a beam of light entering through this energetic portal and infusing your whole being. State – either out loud or internally – that you are available for the download and that you are ready to be of service. Allow whatever words come to you to be spoken. Or you can use this invocation:

'Dear God, I make myself available for the download of my divine blueprint. I make myself available for my divine mission. Dear God, use me … I am your eyes, your ears, your mouth, your hands, your feet, your heart and your breath. I am your servant. And even though I may not yet see clearly, I trust that whatever steps I need to take are being revealed to me as I go about my daily life. Dear God, I am a servant of love … I am available.'

As you say this invocation, allow yourself to open like a vessel. You are not looking to receive answers right now. You are simply making yourself energetically available. That's all you need to do.

As you go about your day, watch out for clues – insights, flashes of inspiration, synchronicities – but don't go searching for them.

SELF-REFLECTION EXERCISE

At the end of each day, it's time to ask yourself those pivotal questions:

✦ Am I motivated by immediate gratification or by making a contribution?

✦ Do I choose fear or do I choose love?

✦ Do I serve ego or do I serve God?

✦ Reflect on all your interactions for the day and then rate yourself for each of the questions on a scale of 1 to 10, with 1 being immediate gratification/fear/ego and 10 being contribution/love/God. Be ruthlessly honest here. The point of this exercise is not to berate yourself or to give yourself a gold medal, but to investigate truthfully.

Then reflect over your day again and write out – for each of these questions – what you could have done differently in your day to make your response a 10!

JOURNAL PAGES

....

....

....

....

....

....

....

....

....

....

....

....

....

....

....

....

....

....

....

....

....

....

....

....

....

....

....

....

....

....

....

....

....

....

....

....

....

....

....

....

....

....

....

....

....

....

....

....

....

....

....

....

....

....

....

....

....

....

....

RESOLUTENESS
The Power to Take Action

There is no change without action; and action can only be taken one step at a time. The decision to take a step is one that needs to be made with each step taken.

This lesson is like a silken thread that joins all the previous ones. I say silken because it is both invisible and invincible. It weaves through each of the facets of your inner radiance and binds them together to create both the irrevocable luminescence and the supreme indestructibility of your diamond-nature. It is this diamond that has the power to shine in the world as an Agent of Change.

The lesson of resoluteness has made the most striking impact on my life. Out of the confusion and uncertainty of my early years, it has carved out a new path in which I am always grounded in the conviction of my divine destiny. This is not some goal-oriented idea of how I want my future to look, but a deep faith in the unfoldment of my purpose. This faith has transformed my previously erratic energy to a steady stream of physical, emotional and mental well-being that is fuelled by the infinite supply of Source.

It means I keep walking through all terrain knowing that wherever I go, God goes with me. Whether I travel over mountain peaks or through valley lows, there is an inner light that is never extinguished. This inner light is the resolve to overcome all inner and outer obstacles for the sake of that which is greater than me. The inner obstacles are the voice of ego: the stories of '*I'm not good enough*', '*I'm not strong enough*', '*I'm not ready*', '*I can't*', '*I won't*', and '*I'll do it some other time*'. The outer obstacles are the face of the world; the challenges I encounter that tell me that life is a struggle, that it's all gone wrong, and that there's no real point in reaching for the stars.

Just like the maras – the dark demons faced by Buddha as he sat under the Bodhi tree – the obstacles we each confront appear to be real, until we realize that the overcoming of obstacles is not a battle, but the meeting of everything shrouded in darkness with the luminosity of awareness. It's the decision to be resolutely present to *what is*, even when there is a habitual pull to look backwards in fear or to look forwards in hope. It's about travelling on your path through life with the innocence of an open heart. It requires the power of responsibility, the power of clarity, the power of surrender, the power of presence, the power of openness, the power of gratitude, the power of forgiveness, and the power of nakedness. These are all qualities not only of your radiantly divine nature but also of the divine radiance of God. This is the meaning of the 23rd Psalm: *'Even though I walk through the valley of the shadow of death, I fear no evil. For You are with me wherever I go.'*

This prayer is a day-by-day and moment-to-moment practice. It's the daily renewal of your resolve that brings resolution to old patterns and clears the way ahead for the re-creation of your reality; and it's the moment-to-moment commitment to open presence that leads to the fulfilment of your soul's destiny. Your destiny could be to sow the seeds of a self-sustaining community, to lead a crusade into the new age, or to be an instrument of peace in the midst of war. Or it could be to raise a child in an environment of unconditional love and conscious creativity. What's important here is to never give up ... to never throw your hands up in the air in despair and say '*I can't do it*'. The shift in motivation from serving ego to serving God is the key that unlocks the power of your resoluteness.

When the cause is greater than the fear, you will inevitably take action. The greater the cause, the more brightly will burn the flame of passion that fuels your actions. This is what's called enthusiasm; it means you are powered by God. You become unstoppable because God is always switched on; there is no place where He is not and there is no time when He is not. God just keeps on saying *yes*. And Creation just keeps on creating. That's why action that has no grounding in awakening is pointless. Without an alignment to Divine Purpose it becomes destructive; this is the hellish condition of today's world. But action that is rooted in awakened consciousness becomes an evolutionary spiral into higher heavenly realms. It's the ascent up the golden staircase in the collective vision.

The action that God is calling you to take may not be as grandiose as saving the world. It may be just one miniscule change in your lifestyle that enhances your well-being. Either way, the magnitude of the resoluteness required is the same. Whatever you're being called to do, the invitation right here and *now* is for you to make a commitment to the journey. If you're honest, you will know what the calling is. Right now, it could be as simple as the completion of the daily lessons in this book.

The commitment is that you will not falter; that

you will apply your full resoluteness to taking each step, even when things get tough; that if you fall off the path, you will get back on. One of the biggest stumbling blocks to making true change in our lives is that when we appear to fall off the path we think we've failed and we lose our resolve. But beating up on yourself for making a mistake moves you even further away from living your life at your highest potential. It's like carrying a bag of old woes uphill – you end up weighed down and demoralized.

I invite you – right here and right *now* – to resolve to have the steadfastness of a warrior and the lightness of an angel. In other words, stand firmly in your decision to walk the path of change, but step lightly so that you do not leave behind any baggage. Life is not a problem to be solved but an adventure to be enjoyed. There is no failure in the eyes of God. All that truly matters is the honest willingness to take the steps … and the courage to try.

It is only by taking the steps to becoming all that you wish to be that you remember you already *are* all that you can be. You always *have* been – and always *will* be – an infinite spiritual being. God knows this is true … and so do you, in your heart of hearts. You may be cloaked in a physical body, but have the resolve to deny the illusion of limitation that your physicality engenders. Choose instead to inhabit the eternal radiance of your essential nature.

You *are* the light of God … and no-one and no-thing can take this away from you, even when you forget. Your job here on Earth is to remember that you are this light. In doing so, you become the light of the world.

DAILY DECLARATION

Repeat 3 times daily

I choose to remember that I AM a spiritual being of infinite magnitude.

I choose to inhabit my eternal radiant nature.

I AM the light of God.

I AM the light of the world.

CALL TO ACTION

Make a commitment to yourself and to God that you will walk on your path with resolute presence and openness. Make a commitment with your whole body, mind and soul that you will have the resolve of a warrior and the lightness of an angel as you take steps towards your divine destiny.

At the end of *each day* this week, describe in your journal how you had the courage to take these steps. Notice where you forgot to take these steps and then choose to re-ignite your commitment to taking them from now on – but do not berate yourself! Simply be a witness to your growth, knowing that everything is unfolding as it should be.

At the *end of this week*, read over your list and congratulate yourself for having the courage to take the steps that you did! Celebrate by doing something very loving towards yourself. Perhaps pamper yourself with a luxurious bath, or go for a long walk, or buy yourself a special treat ... whatever it takes to make you feel enveloped in the arms of God.

SELF-REFLECTION EXERCISE

And finally ... read through your completed journal, week by week, taking a few moments at each stage to reflect on your journey. For each week, make a note in your journal of any thoughts, feelings and new insights that may come to you. Can you feel the changes that are already happening in your life?

JOURNAL PAGES

AFTERWORD
The Next Step

The steps in this book are only the beginning. The invitation is for you to exercise your spiritual muscle until it becomes a natural part of who you are.

Life itself is always inviting you to awaken. Every challenge, every calamity, every loss and every painful situation is calling you to bring the radiance of your love, your compassion, your gratitude and your forgiveness to whatever is happening. What's important here is the recognition that every moment of darkness is pregnant with the light. You now have the tools that enable you to take a deep breath, to relax, and to meet your experience with unwavering presence and unconditional openness. By having taken the steps in this book, you have awakened within you the miracle of your true power … and out of this power is birthed a new you.

Of course, as any mother knows, the process of birth is not always easy. So if you're feeling a little anxious about the journey that unfolds before you, this is to be expected. You are stepping into a radically new life that holds the potential for freedom and fulfilment in ways that perhaps you have never known. Certainly, my journey of awakening has not only taken me to the depths of my own darkness but has also brought me gifts of unimaginable value. One of these gifts is the opportunity to share with you some of the jewels of wisdom that have revealed themselves along the way. I share these in this and other books; also in my talks, teleclasses, workshops and retreats. My invitation is that you join me in a growing global community that is evolving as I evolve … take a look at **www.AmodaMaaJeevan.com** for more details.

You – and I, as well as an increasing percentage of humanity – are also stepping into a radically new world. The collective darkness so many of us are experiencing is a monumentally pregnant moment in the evolutionary journey of our species. It's a moment that holds the potential of a planetary awakening. But it is our capacity to awaken as individuals that will decide how joyful or painful this collective awakening will be. If we choose to take a deep breath, to relax, and to open to the ever-present love that surrounds us, then it's likely we will experience the ecstatic birth of a new way of being … and we will have cause to celebrate. Out of this celebration of ourselves, of the divinity that we share, and of the sacredness of every moment, will be born a new way of living.

My vision is that a new world built on foundations of love will be the driving purpose of our lives, and that we each embrace this purpose with passion and joy. If you are reading this book – and have taken the steps to becoming an Agent of Change – know that you have been called to play an active part in this new world. You have been called to bring your light to the world.

My hope is that you embrace this call and remember that you are the light of God … because that is who you really are.

ADDITIONAL JOURNAL PAGES

....

....

....

....

....

....

....

....

....

....

....

....

....

....

....

....

....

....

....

....

....

....

....

....

....

....

....

....

....

....

....

....